Yellowstone National Park Visitor Study

Winter 2012

Natural Resource Report NPS/NRSS/EQD/NRR— 2012/611

Colleen Kulesza, Yen Le, Steven J. Hollenhorst

Visitor Services Project
Park Studies Unit
University of Idaho
Moscow, ID 83844-1139

December 2012

U.S. Department of the Interior
National Park Service
Natural Resource Stewardship and Science
Fort Collins, Colorado

The National Park Service, Natural Resource Stewardship and Science office in Fort Collins, Colorado, publishes a range of reports that address natural resource topics. These reports are of interest and applicability to a broad audience in the National Park Service and others in natural resource management, including scientists, conservation and environmental constituencies, and the public.

The Natural Resource Report Series is used to disseminate high-priority, current natural resource management information with managerial application. The series targets a general, diverse audience, and may contain NPS policy considerations or address sensitive issues of management applicability.

All manuscripts in the series receive the appropriate level of peer review to ensure that the information is scientifically credible, technically accurate, appropriately written for the intended audience, and designed and published in a professional manner.

Data in this report were collected and analyzed using methods based on established, peer-reviewed protocols and were analyzed and interpreted within the guidelines of the protocols.

Views, statements, findings, conclusions, recommendations, and data in this report do not necessarily reflect views and policies of the National Park Service, U.S. Department of the Interior. Mention of trade names or commercial products does not constitute endorsement or recommendation for use by the U.S. Government.

This report is available from the Social Science Program (http://www.nature.nps.gov/socialscience/index.cfm) and the Natural Resource Publications Management website (http://www.nature.nps.gov/publications/nrpm/).

This report and other reports by the Visitor Services Project (VSP) are available from the VSP website (http://www.psu.uidaho.edu/c5/vsp/vsp-reports/) or by contacting the VSP office at (208) 885-7863.

Please cite this publication as:

Kulesza, C., Y. Le, and S. J. Hollenhorst. 2012. Yellowstone National Park visitor study: Winter 2012. Natural Resource Report NPS/NRSS/EQD/NRR—2012/611. National Park Service, Fort Collins, Colorado.

NPS 101/119336, December 2012

Contents

Page

Executive Summary vii
    Acknowledgements x
    About the Authors x
Introduction 1
    Organization of the Report 1
    Presentation of the Results 2
Methods 3
    Survey Design and Procedures 3
        Sample size and sampling plan 3
        Questionnaire design 3
        Survey procedure 4
        Data analysis 4
        Limitations 5
        Special conditions 5
        Checking non-response bias 6
Results 7
    Group and Visitor Characteristics 7
        Visitor group size 7
        Visitor group type 7
        Visitors with organized groups 8
        United States visitors by state of residence 10
        International visitors by country of residence 11
        Number of visits in past 12 months 12
        Number of lifetime visits 12
        Visitor age 13
        Visitor gender 14
        Visitor ethnicity 14
        Visitor race 14
        Language used for speaking and reading 15
        Translation of services into other languages 16
        Visitors with physical conditions affecting access/participation 17
        Respondent level of education 18
        Respondent household income 19
        Respondent household size 19
    Trip/Visit Characteristics and Preferences 20
        Information sources prior to visit 20
        Information sources for future visit 22
        Park as destination 23
        Resident of the area 23
        Adequacy of directional signs 25
        Number of vehicles used 26
        Number of park entries 26
        Park entrances used 27

Contents (continued)

Page

Overnight stays 27
Old Faithful Snow Lodge.. 28
Mammoth Hotel 29
Accommodations used inside the park 30
Accommodations used outside the park 31
Places stayed on night prior to visit.. 32
Places stayed on night after visit.. 34
Total length of visit... 36
Locations visited 37
Reasons for not visiting locations in the park... 38
Locations not visited in the park 39
Number of hours spent at selected park locations 40
Number of days spent at selected park locations 40
Activities on this visit 41
Activity that was primary reason for visiting Yellowstone NP 43
Ratings of Concession Services and Activities 44
Locating commercial services... 44
Commercial services used in Yellowstone NP 45
Explanation of any "no" and "worse than expected" responses 47
Value of commercial services for money paid 49
Explanation of "very poor" or "poor" ratings of value of commercial services
    for money paid.. 50
Explanation of "very good" ratings of value of commercial services for money
    paid... 52
Planned/reserved concession services and activities 54
Concession services and activities used.. 55
Comparison of concession services and activities planned/reserved vs. used.................. 56
Importance ratings of concession services and activities used 57
Quality ratings of concession services and activities used 58
Expenditures 59
Total expenditures inside and outside the park... 59
Number of adults covered by expenditures 60
Number of children covered by expenditures... 60
Expenditures inside the park 61
Expenditures outside the park 66
Preferences for Future Visits 72
Cell phone service.. 72
Internet access 72
Other services... 72
Overall Quality 73

Contents (continued)

Page

Visitor Comment Summaries 74
    What visitors liked most 74
    What visitors liked least... 76
    Additional comments 78
Visitor Comments... 80
Appendix 1: The Questionnaire 99
Appendix 2: Additional Analysis.. 101
Appendix 3: Decision Rules for Checking Non-response Bias 103
    References.. 104

Executive Summary

This visitor study report profiles a systematic random sample of Yellowstone National Park (NP) visitors during February 15-21, 2012. In total, 433 questionnaires were distributed to visitor groups. Of those, 334 questionnaires were returned, resulting in a 77.1% response rate.

Group size and type
Forty-eight percent of visitor groups consisted of two people and 29% consisted of three or four people. Sixty-three percent of visitor groups consisted of family groups.

State or country of residence
United States visitors were from 48 states and Puerto Rico and comprised 94% of total visitation during the survey period, with 22% from Montana. International visitors were from 13 countries and comprised 6% of total visitation during the survey period, with 21% from Australia.

Frequency of visits
Most visitors (70%) were visiting the park for the first time in the past 12 months and 31% were visiting the park for the first time in their lifetime. Thirty-four percent had visited more than five times in their lifetime.

Age, ethnicity, race, and education
Forty-eight percent of visitors were ages 46-65 years, 12% were 66 or older, and 11% were ages 15 years or younger. One percent were Hispanic or Latino. Ninety-six percent of visitors were White and 2% were Asian. Eighty percent of respondents had a bachelor's degree or graduate degree.

Preferred language
Most visitor groups preferred speaking (97%) and reading (98%) English. Twenty-two percent of visitor groups wanted services provided in another language.

Physical conditions
Five percent of visitor groups had members with physical conditions affecting their ability to access or participate in activities and services.

Household size and income
Sixty percent of households were comprised of two people. Thirteen percent had four people in their household. Thirty-six percent of households had an income of $75,000 to $149,999. Fifteen percent had a household income of $200,000 or more.

Information sources
Ninety percent of visitor groups obtained information about the park prior to their visit through previous visits (63%), the park website (54%), and friends/relatives/word of mouth (53%). Most visitors (97%) received the information they needed. Sixty-seven percent of visitor groups would prefer to use the park website to obtain information for a future visit.

Park as destination
For 64% of visitor groups, the park was the primary destination and for 35%, the park was one of several destinations.

Reason for visiting the park area
Seventeen percent of visitor groups were residents of the area (within 150 miles of the park). Seventy-two percent of visitor groups indicated visiting the park was the primary reason that they visited the area. The most common reasons for visiting the park area were to visit the park (82%) and watch wildlife (64%) and snowmobile/snowcoach (58%).

Transportation and road signs
Eighty-one percent of visitor groups used one vehicle to arrive at the park. Most visitor groups (77%) found the park signs adequate, 71% found state highways signs adequate, and 64% found interstate signs to be adequate.

Executive Summary (continued)

Park entries	Seventy percent of visitor groups entered the park one time during their stay and 18% entered the park twice. Fifty-two percent of the entries were through the West Yellowstone Entrance, 35% were through the North Entrance, and 20% came through the South Entrance.
Overnight stays	Most visitor groups (85%) stayed overnight in the park or in the area within 150 miles of the park. Of those that stayed in the park, 29% stayed five or more nights and 28% stayed two nights. Thirty-one percent stayed five or more nights outside the park in the area (within 150 miles of the park).
Accommodations	Ninety-six percent of visitor groups that stayed in the park and 86% of visitor groups that stayed in the park area used a lodge, hotel, motel, cabin, rented condo/home, or B&B.
Length of visit	Of the visitor groups that spent less than 24 hours in the park, the average length of stay was 7.7 hours. Of the visitor groups that spent 24 hours or more, the average length of stay was 3.8 days. The average length of stay for all visitor groups was 45.6 hours, or 2 days.
Locations visited in the park	Eighty-eight percent of visitor groups visited all the locations in the park that they had planned to visit. Seventy-nine percent of visitor groups visited Old Faithful, 41% visited Madison, and 38% visited Mammoth Hot Springs.
Time spent at park sites	The most common length of time spent at each location was 1-2 hours. Twenty-seven percent of visitor groups spent five or more hours at Mammoth Hot Springs. The highest average number of days spent was three days at Mammoth Hot Springs and Old Faithful.
Activities on this visit	The most common activities were viewing wildlife/birdwatching (86%), boardwalk/geyser basin (77%), and eating in park restaurants (66%). Sixty-three percent of visitor groups took a snowcoach tour on this trip and 22% took a snowmobile tour.
Primary reason for visiting the park	Twenty-six percent of visitor groups listed a snowcoach tour as their primary reason for visiting the park, while 23% listed a snowmobile tour.
Locating commercial services	Three percent of visitor groups indicated that they had difficulty finding commercial services.
Commercial services used	Seventy-one percent of visitor groups ate at a restaurant or used other food services and 55% took a snowcoach tour. Fifty percent of visitor groups used lodging.
Rating commercial services	Almost all visitor groups were able to get their first choice of food services (96%) and lodging (92%). Most visitor groups also indicated that services/ activities met their expectations, while 8% or less of each service/activity was rated "worse than expected."

Executive Summary (continued)

**Value for money
paid for concession
services**

The concession services that received the highest combined "very good" and "good" ratings of value for money paid were snowcoach tour (77%), snowmobile tour (75%), and lodging (74%).

**Concession
services and
activities**

Ninety-two percent of visitor groups were able to use the services/activities that they had planned prior to visiting the park. Specifically, 99% planned to participate in a snowcoach tour (95% did participate), 58% planned a snowmobile tour (93% did), 15% planned a cross-country ski tour (73% did), and 12% planned to rent ski equipment (92% did).

Expenditures

The average visitor group expenditure (inside and outside the park within 150 miles) was $2114. The median group expenditure (50% of groups spent more and 50% of groups spent less) was $1197, and the average total expenditure per person (per capita) was $777.

**Technology access
on future visits**

Sixty-one percent of visitor groups would like to have cell phone access in developed areas of the park on future visits. Forty-nine percent of visitor groups would like to have internet access.

Overall quality

Most visitor groups (94%) rated the overall quality of facilities, services, and recreational opportunities at Yellowstone NP as "very good" or "good." One percent of groups rated the overall quality as "very poor" or "poor."

For more information about the Visitor Services Project, please contact the Park Studies Unit at the University of Idaho at (208) 885-7863 or the following website http://www.psu.uidaho.edu.

Acknowledgements

We thank Colleen Kulesza for compiling the report, Margaret Littlejohn for overseeing the fieldwork, George Helfrich and the staff and volunteers of Yellowstone National Park for assisting with the survey, and David Vollmer and Matthew Strawn for data processing.

About the Authors

Colleen Kulesza is a doctoral candidate at the University of Idaho and a research assistant for the Visitor Services Project. Yen Le, Ph.D., is Assistant Director of the Visitor Services Project at the University of Idaho, and Steven Hollenhorst, Ph.D., was the Director of the Park Studies Unit, Department of Conservation Social Sciences, University of Idaho.

Introduction

This report describes the results of a visitor study at Yellowstone National Park (NP) in Wyoming, conducted February 15-21, 2012 by the National Park Service (NPS) Visitor Services Project (VSP), part of the Park Studies Unit (PSU) at the University of Idaho.

As described in the National Park Service website for Yellowstone NP, "…the park was established in 1872 as America's first national park—an idea that spread worldwide. A mountain wildland, home to grizzly bears, wolves, and herds of bison and elk, the park is the core of one of the last, nearly intact, natural ecosystems in the Earth's temperate zone." (www.nps.gov/yell, retrieved April 2012).

Organization of the Report

This report is organized into three sections.

Section 1: **Methods**. This section discusses survey methodology procedures, limitations, and special conditions that may affect the study results.

Section 2: **Results**. This section provides a summary for each question in the questionnaire and includes visitor comments to open-ended questions. The presentation of the results of this study does not follow the order of questions in the questionnaire.

Section 3: **Appendices**
Appendix 1: *The Questionnaire*. A copy of the questionnaire distributed to visitor groups.

Appendix 2: *Additional Analysis.* A list of sample questions for cross-references and cross comparisons. Comparisons can be analyzed within a park or between parks. Results of additional analyses are not included in this report.

Appendix 3: *Decision Rules for Checking Non-response Bias.* An explanation of how the non-response bias was determined.

Presentation of the Results

Results are represented in the form of graphs (see example 1), scatter plots, pie charts, tables, and text.

EXAMPLE KEY

1. The figure title describes the graph's information.

2. Listed above the graph, the "N" shows the number of individuals or visitor groups responding to the question. If "N" is less than 30, "**CAUTION!**" is shown on the graph to indicate the results may be unreliable.

* appears when the total percentages do not equal 100 due to rounding.

** appears when total percentages do not equal 100 because visitors could select more than one answer choice.

3. Vertical information describes the response categories.

4. Horizontal information shows the number or proportion of responses in each category.

5. In most graphs, percentages provide additional information.

EXAMPLE 1

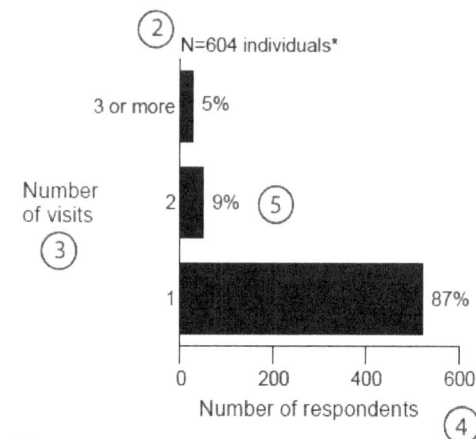

Figure 14. Number of visits to the park in past 12 months

Methods

Survey Design and Procedures

Sample size and sampling plan

All VSP questionnaires follow design principles outlined in Don A. Dillman's book *Mail and Internet Surveys: The Tailored Design Method* (2007). Using this method, the sample size was calculated based on the park's visitation statistics of previous years.

Brief interviews were conducted with a systematic, random sample of visitor groups that arrived at three sites during February 15-21, 2012. Visitors were surveyed between the hours of 8 a.m. and 7 p.m. Table 1 shows the three locations and for each location, the number of questionnaires distributed and response rate. During this survey, 506 visitor groups were contacted and 433 of these groups (85.6%) accepted questionnaires. (The average acceptance rate for 250 VSP visitor studies conducted from 1988 through 2011 is 91.5%.) Questionnaires were completed and returned by 334 respondents, resulting in a 77.1% response rate for this study. (The average response rate for the 250 VSP visitor studies is 72.3%.)

Table 1. Questionnaire distribution, winter 2012
(N=number of questionnaires)

Sampling site	Distributed		Returned	
	N	%	N	%
West Entrance	207	48	166	80
Mammoth	127	29	101	80
Flagg Ranch	99	23	67	68
Total	433	100%	334	

Questionnaire design

The Yellowstone NP questionnaire was developed through conference calls between the park and the VSP staff to design and prioritize questions. Some of the questions are comparable with VSP studies conducted at other parks while others were customized for Yellowstone NP. Many questions ask respondents to choose answers from a list of responses, often with an open-ended option, while others are completely open-ended.

No pilot study was conducted to test the Yellowstone NP questionnaire. However, all questions followed Office Management and Budget (OMB) guidelines and/or were used in previous surveys; thus the clarity and consistency of the survey instrument has been tested and supported.

Survey procedure

Visitor groups were greeted, briefly introduced to the purpose of the study, and asked to participate. If visitors agreed, they were asked which member (at least 16 years old) had the next birthday. The individual with the next birthday was selected to complete the questionnaire for the group. An interview, lasting approximately two minutes, was conducted with that person to determine group size, group type, the age of the member completing the questionnaire, and how this visit to the park fit into their group's travel plans. These individuals were asked their names, addresses, and telephone numbers or email addresses in order to mail them a reminder/thank-you postcard and follow-ups. Participants were asked to complete the survey after their visit and mail it using the Business Reply Mail envelope provided.

Two weeks following the survey, a reminder/thank-you postcard was mailed to all participants who provided a valid mailing address (see Table 2). Replacement questionnaires were mailed to participants who had not returned their questionnaires four weeks after the survey. Seven weeks after the survey, a second round of replacement questionnaires was mailed to participants who had not returned their questionnaires.

Table 2. Follow-up mailing distribution

Mailing	Date	U.S.	International	Total
Postcards	March 7, 2012	404	25	429
1st replacement	March 21, 2012	170	15	185
2nd replacement	April 11, 2012	135	0	135

Data analysis

Returned questionnaires were coded and the responses were processed using custom and standard statistical software applications—Statistical Analysis Software® (SAS), and a custom designed FileMaker Pro® application. Descriptive statistics and cross-tabulations were calculated for the coded data; responses to open-ended questions were categorized and summarized. Double-key data entry validation was performed on numeric and text entry variables and the remaining checkbox (bubble) variables were read by optical mark recognition (OMR) software.

Limitations

As with all surveys, this study has limitations that should be considered when interpreting the results.

1. This was a self-administered survey. Respondents completed the questionnaire after their visit, which may have resulted in poor recall. Thus, it is not possible to know whether visitor responses reflected actual behavior.

2. The data reflect visitor use patterns at the selected sites during the study period of February 15-21, 2012. The results present a 'snapshot in time' and do not necessarily apply to visitors during other times of the year.

3. Caution is advised when interpreting any data with a sample size of less than 30, as the results may be unreliable. When the sample size is less than 30, the word "**CAUTION!**" is included in the graph, figure, table, or text.

4. Occasionally, there may be inconsistencies in the results. Inconsistencies arise from missing data or incorrect answers (due to misunderstood directions, carelessness, or poor recall of information). Therefore, refer to both the percentage and N (number of individuals or visitor groups) when interpreting the results.

Special conditions

The temperatures during the survey period varied from 10F to 20F. It was often overcast with occasional snowfall and sunny periods. The duration of the survey encompassed President's Day weekend so could have had an affect on visitation.

Checking non-response bias

Five variables were used to check non-response bias: participant age, group size, group type, park as destination, and participant proximity from home to the park. All variables were found to be insignificantly different between respondents and non-respondents except for average age and proximity from home to the park (see Tables 3 - 6). Respondents of younger age ranges (especially 40 and younger) may be underrepresented in the results. Visitors who lived within a 200 mile radius of the park may also be underrepresented. See Appendix 3 for more details of the non-response bias checking procedures.

Table 3. Comparison of respondents and non-respondents by average age and group size

Variable	Respondents	Non-respondents	p-value (t-test)
Age (years)	52.73 (N=333)	45.74 (N=94)	<0.001
Group size	3.44 (N=893)	3.74 (N=98)	0.319

Table 4. Comparison of respondents and non-respondents by group type

Group type	Respondents	Non-respondents	p-value (chi-square)
Alone	16	7	
Family	207	57	
Friends	53	15	
Family and friends	51	17	
Other	2	1	
			0.848

Table 5. Comparison of respondents and non-respondents by primary destination

Destination	Respondents	Non-respondents	p-value (chi-square)
Park as primary destination	218	55	
Park as one of several destinations	106	44	
Unplanned visit	4	0	
			0.093

Table 6. Comparison of respondents and non-respondents by distance from home to park

Distance	Respondents	Non-respondents	p-value (chi-square)
Within 200 miles	74	14	
201-400 miles	37	8	
401-600 miles	38	4	
601 miles or more	166	59	
International visitors	14	11	
			0.004

Results

Group and Visitor Characteristics

Visitor group size

Question 17b
On this visit, how many people, including yourself, were in your personal group?

Results
- 48% of visitor groups consisted of two people (see Figure 1).

- 29% were in groups of three or four.

- 13% were in groups with six or more.

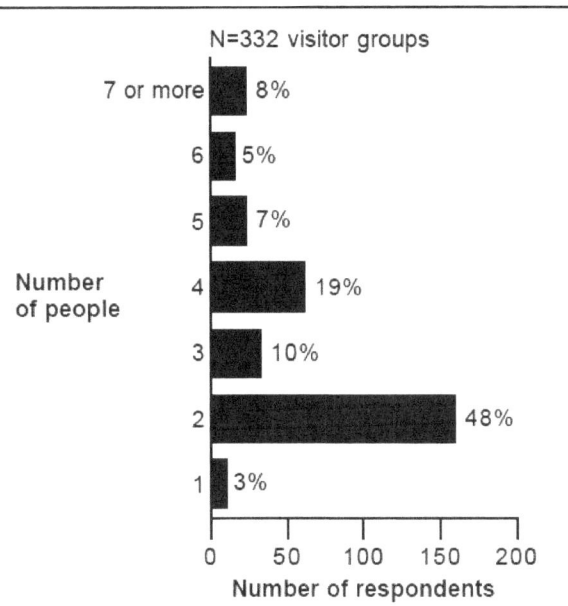

Figure 1. Visitor group size

Visitor group type

Question 17a
On this visit, what type of personal group (not guided tour/school/other organized group) were you with?

Results
- 63% of visitor groups consisted of family members (see Figure 2).

- "Other" group type (1%) was:

    Graduate school advisors

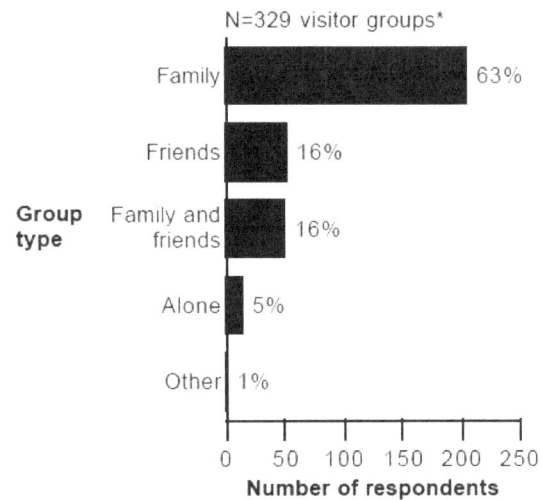

Figure 2. Visitor group type

7

Visitors with organized groups

Question 16a

On this visit, was your personal group with a commercial guided tour group?

Results
*   44% of visitor groups were with a commercial guided tour group (see Figure 3).

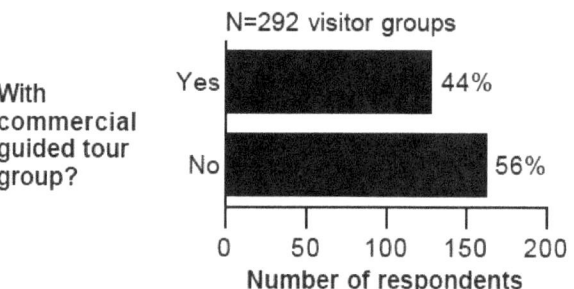

Figure 3. Visitors with a commercial guided tour group

Question 16b

On this visit, was your personal group with a school/educational group?

Results
*   1% of visitor groups were with a school/educational group (see Figure 4).

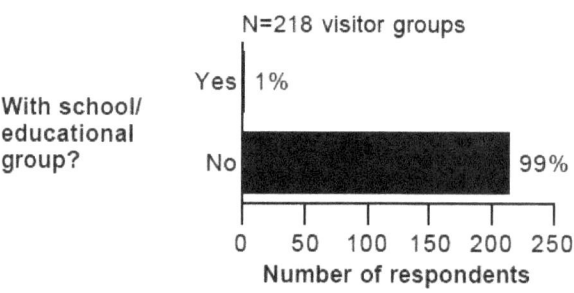

Figure 4. Visitors with a school/educational group

Question 16c

On this visit, was your personal group with an "other" organized group (business, church, scouts, work)?

Results
*   5% of visitor groups were with an "other" organized group (see Figure 5).

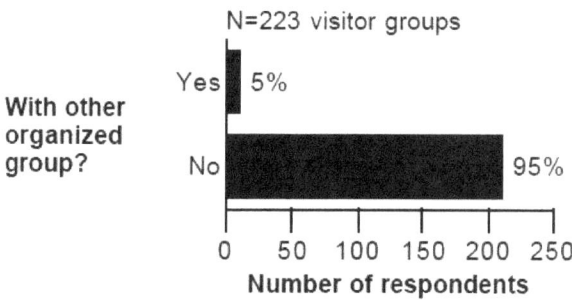

Figure 5. Visitors with an "other" organized group

*total percentages do not equal 100 due to rounding

**total percentages do not equal 100 because visitors could select more than one answer

Question 16d

If you were with one of these organized groups, how many people, including yourself, were in this group?

Results

- 60% of visitor groups who traveled with an organized group were composed of 1-10 people (see Figure 6).

- 25% consisted of 11-20 people.

- 12% consisted of 21-30 people.

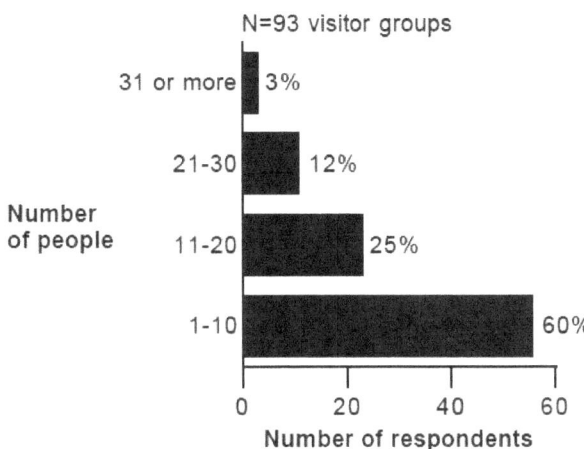

Figure 6. Organized group size

*total percentages do not equal 100 due to rounding
**total percentages do not equal 100 because visitors could select more than one answer

9

United States visitors by state of residence

Question 18c

For your personal group on this visit, what is your state of residence?

Note: Response was limited to seven members from each visitor group.

Results

- U.S. visitors were from 48 states and Puerto Rico and comprised 94% of total visitation to the park during the survey period.

- 22% of U.S. visitors were from Montana, 7% were from Utah and 7% were from California (see Table 7 and Figure 7).

- Smaller proportions came from 45 other states and Puerto Rico.

Table 7. United States visitors by state of residence

State	Number of visitors	Percent of U.S. visitors N=894 individuals*	Percent of total visitors N=947 individuals
Montana	201	22	21
Utah	64	7	7
California	59	7	6
Wyoming	41	5	4
Colorado	40	4	4
Washington	39	4	4
Georgia	34	4	4
New York	32	4	3
Connecticut	21	2	2
Michigan	21	2	2
Minnesota	20	2	2
Ohio	20	2	2
Tennessee	19	2	2
Wisconsin	19	2	2
Texas	18	2	2
Idaho	17	2	2
Indiana	17	2	2
North Carolina	15	2	2
Pennsylvania	15	2	2
Illinois	14	2	1
New Jersey	14	2	1
27 other states and Puerto Rico	149	17	16

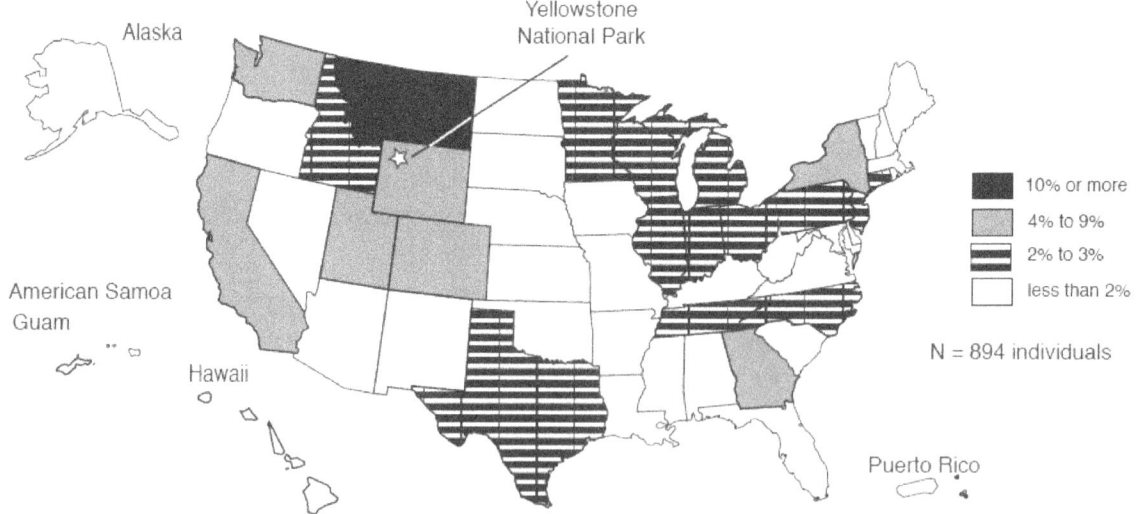

Figure 7. United States visitors by state of residence

---

*total percentages do not equal 100 due to rounding

**total percentages do not equal 100 because visitors could select more than one answer

International visitors by country of residence

Question 18c

For your personal group on this visit, what is your country of residence?

Note: Response was limited to seven members from each visitor group.

Results
- International visitors were from 13 countries and comprised 6% of total visitation to the park during the survey period.

- 21% of international visitors came from Australia (see Table 8).

- 19% came from the United Kingdom.

- 15% came from the Netherlands.

- 11% came from Germany.

- Smaller proportions of international visitors came from 9 other countries.

Table 8. International visitors by country of residence

Country	Number of visitors	Percent of international visitors N=53 individuals*	Percent of total visitors N=947 individuals
Australia	11	21	1
United Kingdom	10	19	1
Netherlands	8	15	1
Germany	6	11	1
Canada	3	6	<1
Japan	3	6	<1
Belgium	2	4	<1
France	2	4	<1
Italy	2	4	<1
New Zealand	2	4	<1
Switzerland	2	4	<1
Austria	1	2	<1
South Africa	1	2	<1

*total percentages do not equal 100 due to rounding
**total percentages do not equal 100 because visitors could select more than one answer

Number of visits in past 12 months

Question 18d

For your personal group on this visit, how many times have you visited Yellowstone NP in the past 12 months (including this visit)?

Note: Response was limited to seven members from each visitor group.

Results

- 70% of visitors visited the park once in the past 12 months (see Figure 8).

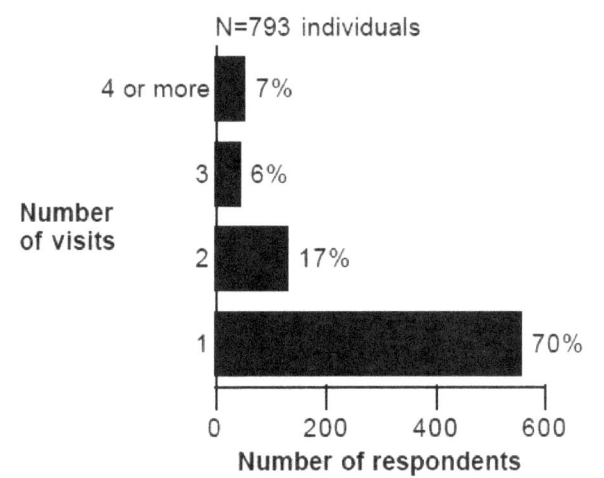

Figure 8. Number of visits to park in past 12 months

Number of lifetime visits

Question 18e

For your personal group on this visit, how many times have you visited Yellowstone NP in your lifetime (including this visit)?

Note: Response was limited to seven members from each visitor group.

Results

- 34% of visitors had visited the park five or more times in the their lifetime (see Figure 9).

- 31% visited the park for the first time.

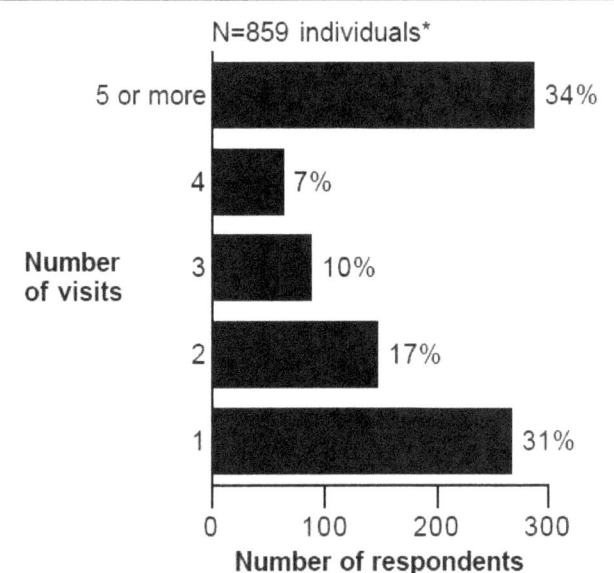

Figure 9. Number of visits to park in lifetime

*total percentages do not equal 100 due to rounding
**total percentages do not equal 100 because visitors could select more than one answer

Visitor age

Question 18b

For your personal group on this visit, what is your current age?

Note: Response was limited to seven members from each visitor group.

Results

- Visitor ages ranged from 1 to 84 years.

- 48% of visitors were 46 to 65 years old (see Figure 10).

- 12% were 66 years or older.

- 11% were 15 years or younger.

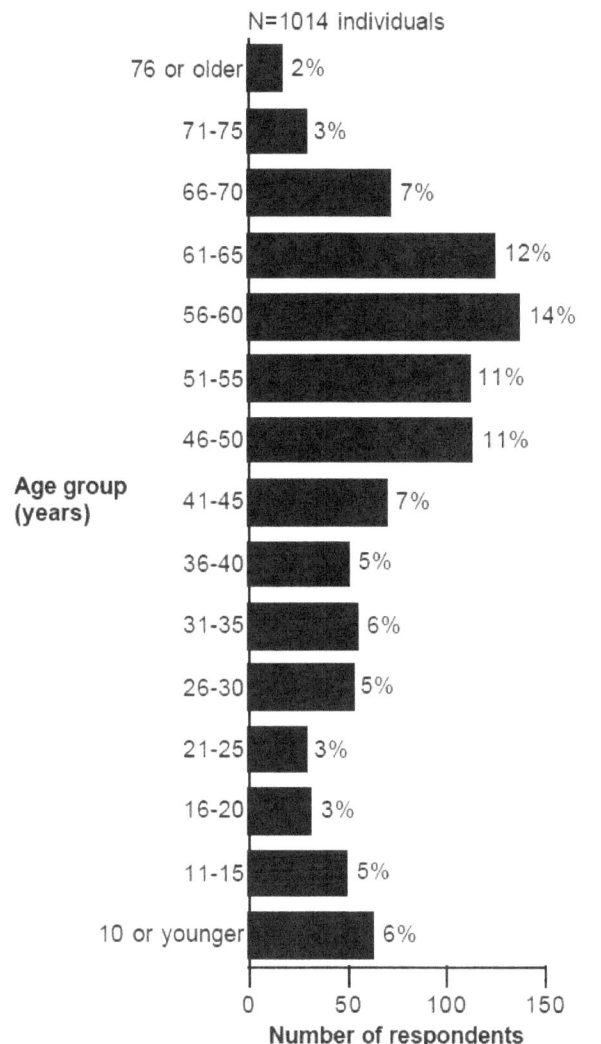

N=1014 individuals

Age group (years)

Number of respondents

Figure 10. Visitor age

*total percentages do not equal 100 due to rounding
**total percentages do not equal 100 because visitors could select more than one answer

13

Visitor gender

Question 18a
For your personal group on this visit, what is your gender?

Note: Response was limited to seven members from each visitor group.

Results
- 51% of respondents were female (see Figure 11).

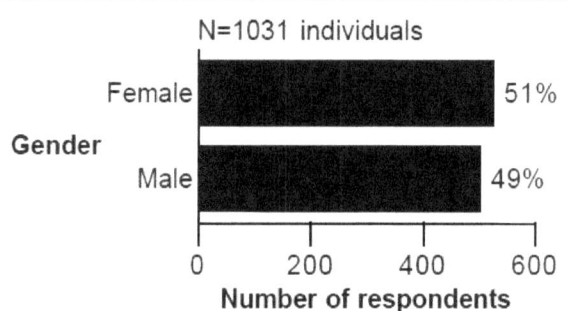

Figure 11. Visitor gender

Visitor ethnicity

Question 22a
Are members of your personal group Hispanic or Latino?

Note: Response was limited to seven members from each visitor group.

Results
- 1% of visitors were Hispanic or Latino (see Figure 12).

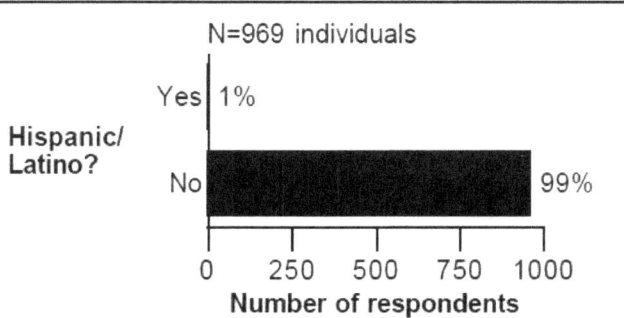

Figure 12. Visitors who were Hispanic or Latino

Visitor race

Question 22b
What is the race of each member of your personal group?

Note: Response was limited to seven members from each visitor group.

Results
- 96% of visitors were White (see Figure 13).

- 2% were Asian.

- 1% were American Indian or Alaska Native.

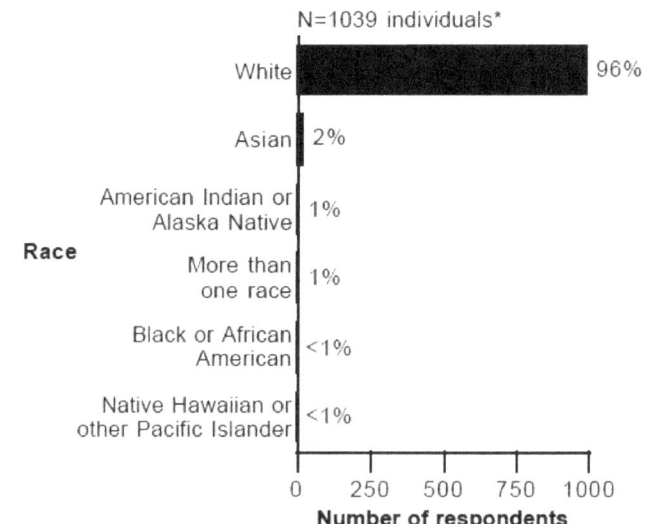

Figure 13. Visitor race

---

*total percentages do not equal 100 due to rounding

**total percentages do not equal 100 because visitors could select more than one answer

Language used for speaking and reading

Question 20a

When visiting an area such as Yellowstone NP, which language(s) do most members of your personal group prefer to use for speaking?

Results

*   97% of visitor groups preferred English for speaking (see Figure 14).

*   Other languages (2%) are listed in Table 9.

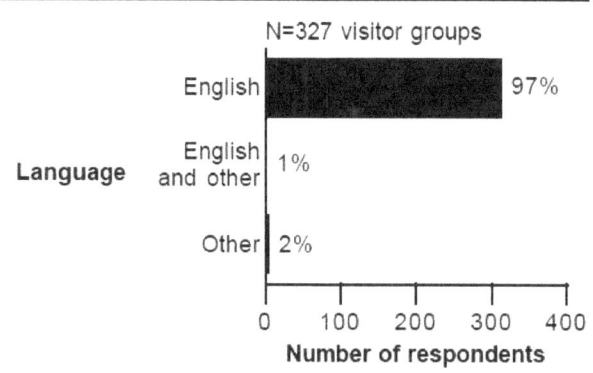

N=327 visitor groups

Figure 14. Language preferred for speaking

Question 20b

When visiting an area such as Yellowstone NP, which language(s) do most members of your personal group prefer to use for reading?

Results

*   98% of visitor groups preferred English for reading (see Figure 15).

*   Other languages (1%) are listed in Table 10.

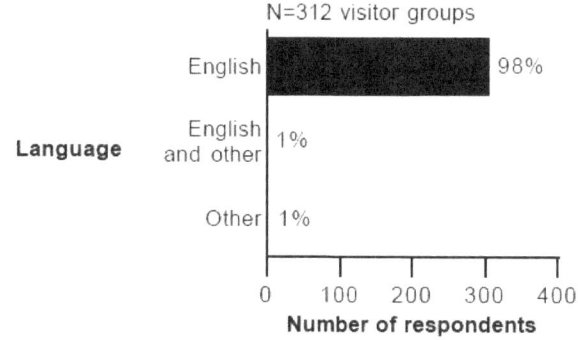

N=312 visitor groups

Figure 15. Language preferred for reading

Table 9. Other languages preferred for speaking (N=9 comments) – **CAUTION!**

Language	Number of times mentioned
French	3
German	2
Afrikaans	1
Dutch	1
Japanese	1
Swiss German	1

Table 10. Other languages preferred for reading (N=4 comments) – **CAUTION!**

Language	Number of times mentioned
Afrikaans	1
French	1
Japanese	1
Swiss German	1

*total percentages do not equal 100 due to rounding

**total percentages do not equal 100 because visitors could select more than one answer

Translation of services into other languages

Question 20c

What services in the park need to be provided in languages other than English? (Open ended)

Results

- 22% of visitor groups would like to have services provided in languages other than English (see Figure 16).

- Table 11 shows the services that visitor groups would like to have provided in languages other than English.

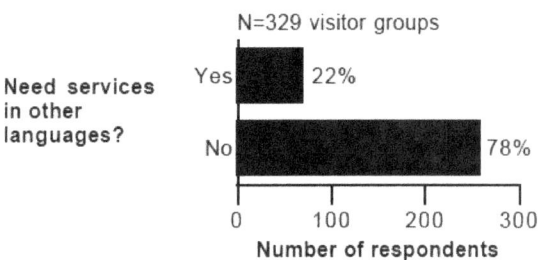

N=329 visitor groups

Figure 16. Visitor groups that would like to have services provided in other languages

Table 11. Services needing translation to other languages (N=27 comments) – **CAUTION!**

Service	Number of times mentioned
All	3
Geyser danger signs	2
Interpretive services	2
Medical services	2
Most staff should be bilingual	2
Park map	2
Safety signs	2
Signs	2
Brochures	1
Directions	1
Exhibits	1
Front desk	1
Interpretive signs	1
Literature	1
Lodging information	1
Menus, snack shop signs	1
Restrooms, gas, food signs	1
Visitors center (texts)	1

*total percentages do not equal 100 due to rounding
**total percentages do not equal 100 because visitors could select more than one answer

Visitors with physical conditions affecting access/participation

Question 21a

Does anyone in your personal group have a physical condition that made it difficult to access or participate in park activities or services?

Results

- 5% of visitor groups had members with physical conditions affecting access or participation in park activities or services (see Figure 17).

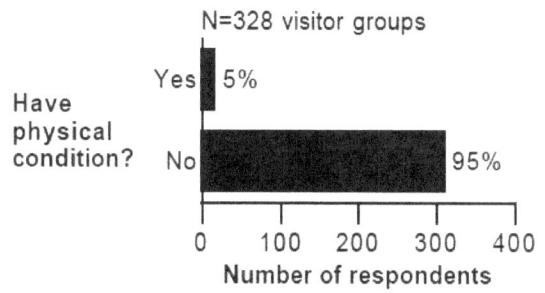

Figure 17. Visitor groups that had members with physical conditions affecting access or participation in park activities or services

Question 21b

If YES, what services or activities were difficult to access/participate in? (Open-ended)

Results

- The services/activities that were difficult for some visitor groups to access/participate in are listed below in Table 12.

Table 12. Services/activities that were difficult to access/participate in (N=16 comments) – **CAUTION!**

Service/activity	Number of times mentioned
Getting out to certain snow covered areas	2
Anything involving walking	1
Breathing	1
Geyser/danger signs	1
Geyser trail at Old Faithful	1
Paths at Old Faithful not shoveled and cleaned	1
Restrooms in Mammoth Lodge	1
Skiing	1
Snowcoach	1
Snowmobiles	1
Snowshoeing	1
Trails with any incline	1
Undine Falls	1
Visitor center exhibits	1
Wintertime snow difficult for crutches	1

*total percentages do not equal 100 due to rounding

**total percentages do not equal 100 because visitors could select more than one answer

Question 21c
Because of the physical condition, which specific difficulties did the person(s) have?

Results – Interpret results with **CAUTION!**
- Not enough visitor groups responded to this question to provide reliable results (see Figure 18).

- "Other" specific problems (27%) encountered by visitor groups were:

         Need oxygen
         Out of breath
         Small seats

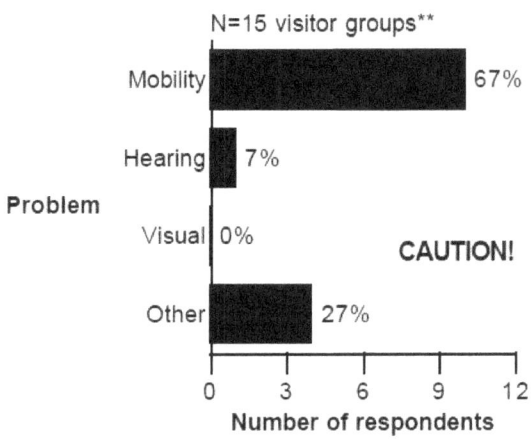

Figure 18. Specific problems encountered by visitors with physical conditions affecting access/participation

Respondent level of education

Question 19
For you only, what is the highest level of education you have completed?

Results
- 42% of respondents had a graduate degree (see Figure 19).

- 38% had a bachelor's degree.

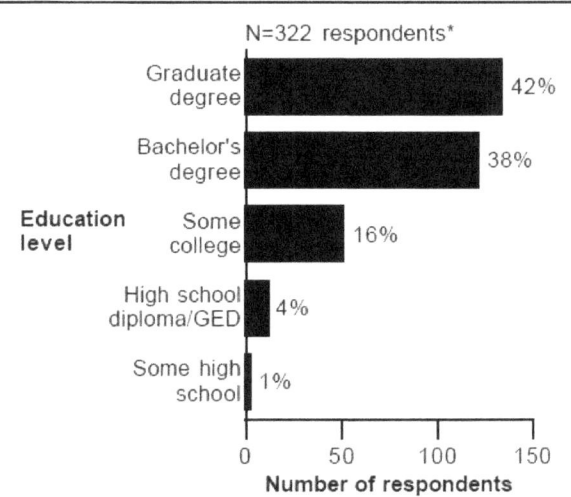

Figure 19. Respondent level of education

---

*total percentages do not equal 100 due to rounding
**total percentages do not equal 100 because visitors could select more than one answer

Respondent household income

Question 23a

Which category best represents your annual household income?

Results

- 20% of respondents reported a household income of $100,000-$149,999 (see Figure 20).

- 16% had an income of $75,000-$99,999.

- 15% had an income of $200,000 or more.

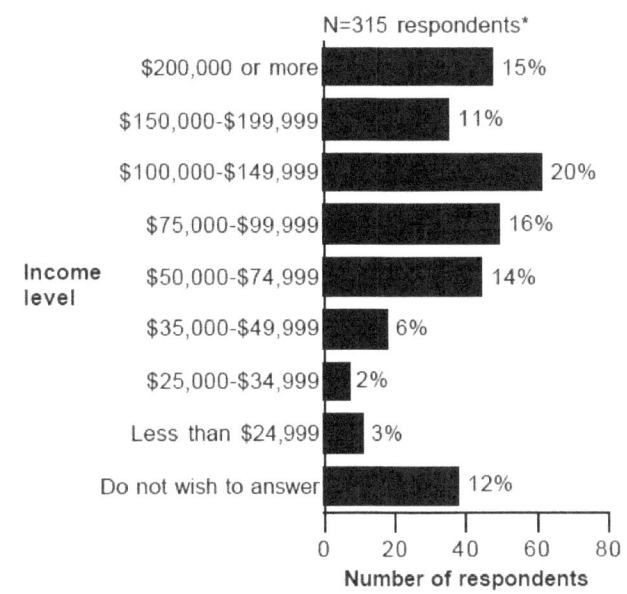

Figure 20. Respondent household income

Respondent household size

Question 23b

How many people are in your household?

Results

- 60% of respondents had two people in their household (see Figure 21).

- 13% had four people.

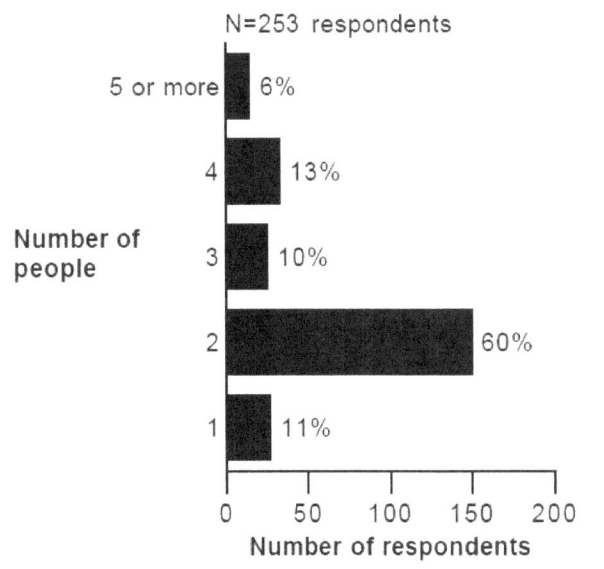

Figure 21. Number of people in respondent household

---

*total percentages do not equal 100 due to rounding

**total percentages do not equal 100 because visitors could select more than one answer

Trip/Visit Characteristics and Preferences

Information sources prior to visit

Question 1a

Prior to this visit, how did your personal group obtain information about Yellowstone NP?

Results

- 90% of visitor groups obtained information about Yellowstone NP prior to their visit (see Figure 22).

- As shown in Figure 23, among those visitor groups that obtained information about Yellowstone NP prior to their visit, the most common sources were:

  63% Previous visits
  54% Yellowstone NP website
  53% Friends/relatives/word of mouth

- Other sources (7%) were:

  Commercial tour company
  International Wolf Federation
  iPad app
  National Geographic
  Travel agent
  Travel show and state fair
  Worked at park previously
  Yellowstone Association

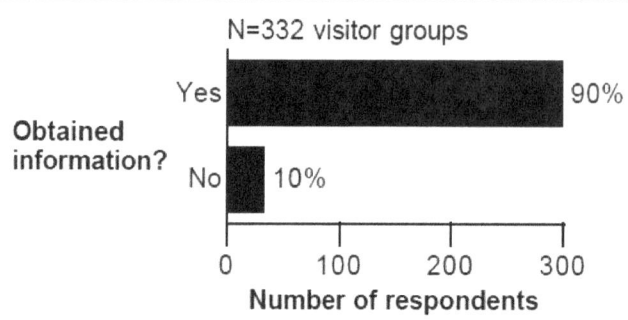

Figure 22. Visitor groups that obtained information prior to visit

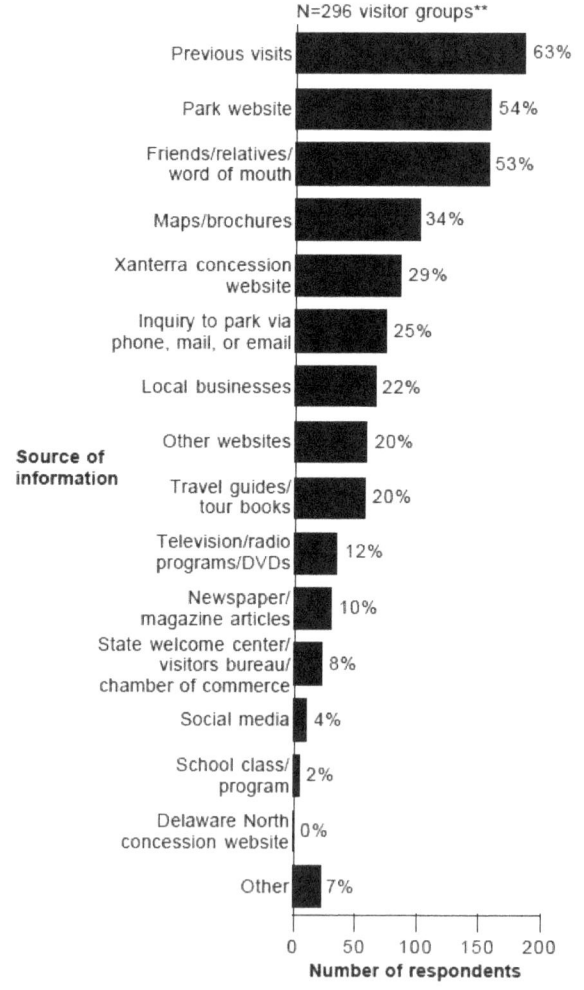

Figure 23. Sources of information used by visitor groups prior to visit

---

*total percentages do not equal 100 due to rounding

**total percentages do not equal 100 because visitors could select more than one answer

Question 1c

From the sources you used prior to this visit, did your personal group receive the type of information about the park that you needed?

Results

- 97% of visitor groups received needed information prior to their visit (see Figure 24).

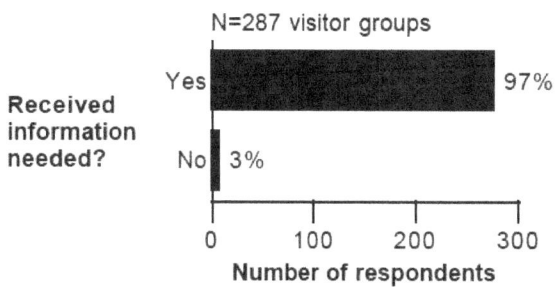

N=287 visitor groups

Figure 24. Visitor groups that received needed information prior to their visit

Question 1d

If NO, what type of park information did your personal group need that was not available? (Open-ended)

Results – Interpret results with **CAUTION!**

- 9 visitor groups listed information they needed but was not available (see Table 13).

Table 13. Needed information that was not available (N=9 comments) – **CAUTION!**

Information	Number of times mentioned
Better ski maps of Old Faithful area	1
Description of Xanterra tours not clear	1
Incorrect advice about room facilities	1
Only received a map - would have liked a detailed booklet about different areas	1
Ski, snowshoe rentals at Old Faithful	1
Snow conditions for cross country skiing not available	1
Specifics about entry to the park and costs	1
Was not aware park roads in North were drivable	1
We wanted more facts on the park from our guide	1

*total percentages do not equal 100 due to rounding
**total percentages do not equal 100 because visitors could select more than one answer

Information sources for future visit

Question 1b

If you were to visit Yellowstone NP in the future, how would your personal group prefer to obtain information about the park?

Results

- As shown in Figure 25, visitor groups' preferred sources of information for a future visit were:

    67% Yellowstone NP website
    58% Previous visits
    37% Maps/brochures

- Other sources of information (2%) were:

    Commercial tour company
    Fishing guide

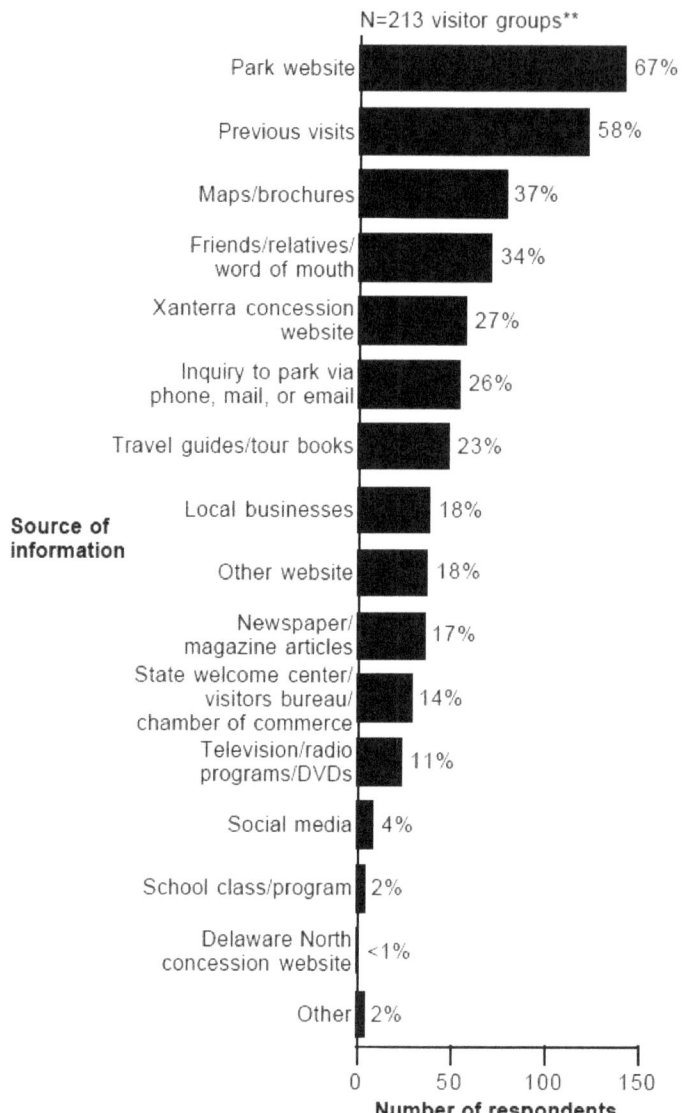

Source of information

N=213 visitor groups**

Source	%
Park website	67%
Previous visits	58%
Maps/brochures	37%
Friends/relatives/word of mouth	34%
Xanterra concession website	27%
Inquiry to park via phone, mail, or email	26%
Travel guides/tour books	23%
Local businesses	18%
Other website	18%
Newspaper/magazine articles	17%
State welcome center/visitors bureau/chamber of commerce	14%
Television/radio programs/DVDs	11%
Social media	4%
School class/program	2%
Delaware North concession website	<1%
Other	2%

Number of respondents

Figure 25. Sources of information to use for a future visit

Park as destination

Question from on-site interview

A two-minute interview was conducted with each individual selected to complete the questionnaire. During the interview, the question was asked: "How did this visit to Yellowstone NP fit into your personal group's travel plans?"

Results

- 64% of visitor groups indicated that Yellowstone National Park was their primary destination (see Figure 26).

- 35% indicated the park was one of several destinations.

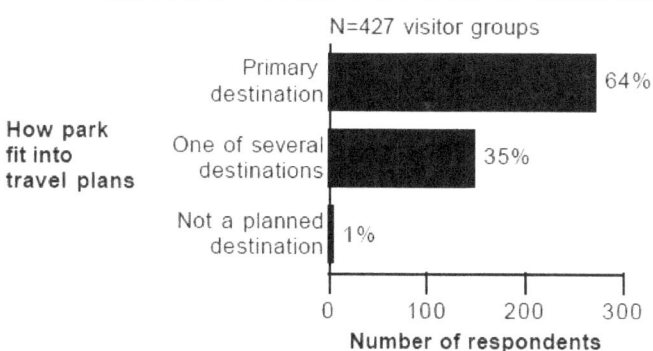

Figure 26. How visit to park fit into visitor groups' travel plans

Resident of the area

Question 10a

Were all members of your personal group residents of the Yellowstone NP area (within 150 miles of the park)?

Results

- 17% of visitor groups were residents of the area (see Figure 27).

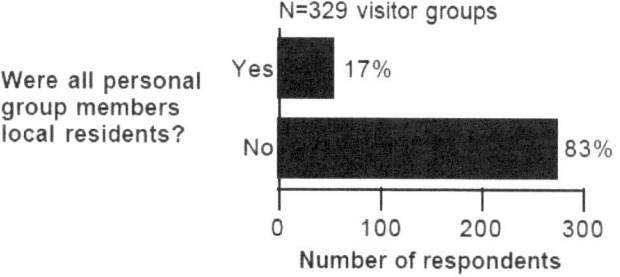

Figure 27. Residents of the area (within 150 miles of the park)

Reason for visiting the area

Question 10b

For this trip, was visiting Yellowstone NP the primary reason that your personal group visited the area (within 150 miles of the park)?

Results

- 72% of visitor groups indicated that visiting Yellowstone NP was the primary reason that they visited the area (see Figure 28).

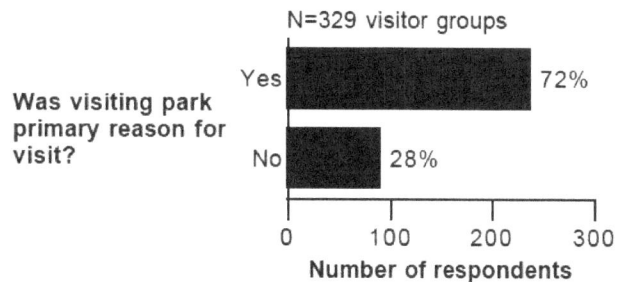

Figure 28. Primary reason for visit

*total percentages do not equal 100 due to rounding

**total percentages do not equal 100 because visitors could select more than one answer

Question 2

For this trip, what are the reasons your personal group visited the Yellowstone NP area (within 150 miles of the park)?

Results

- As shown in Figure 29, the most common reasons for visiting the Yellowstone NP area (within 150 miles) among groups were:

  82% Visit the park
  64% Watch wildlife
  58% Snowmobiling/ snowcoach
  47% Snowshoeing/skiing

- Other reasons (7%) were:

  Dog sledding
  Family vacation
  Guest ranch
  Hiking
  Live in West Yellowstone
  Part of package tour
  Photography
  Photography tour/workshop
  Purchased at a fundraising event
  See Yellowstone in winter
  Sightseeing
  Snowmobiling
  Staying at second home in Big Sky
  Traveling through - planned visit
  Winter fly-fishing
  Won a commercial tour trip

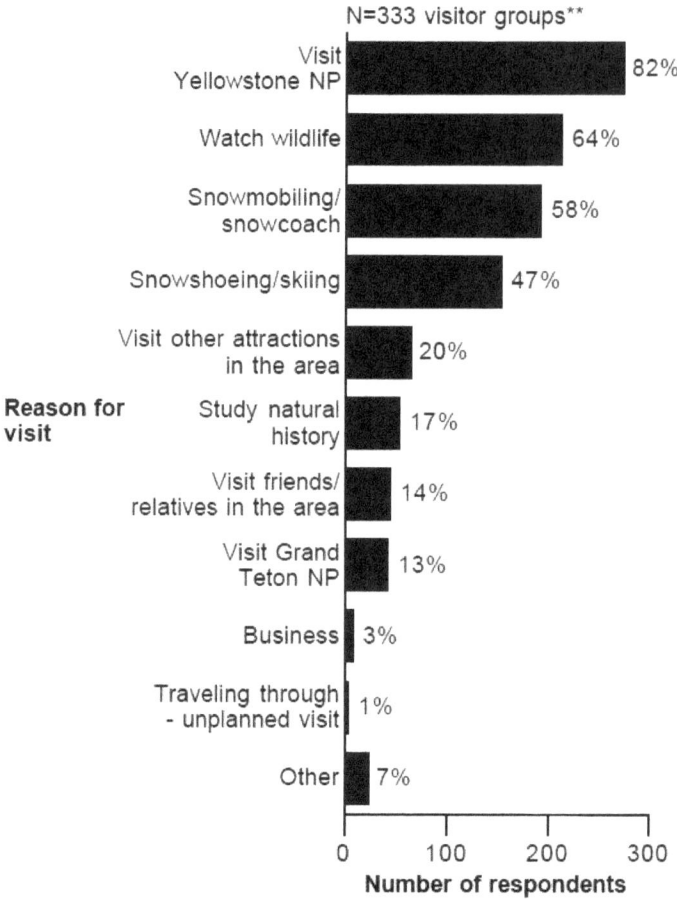

Figure 29. Reasons for visiting the Yellowstone NP area (within 150 miles of the park)

*total percentages do not equal 100 due to rounding
**total percentages do not equal 100 because visitors could select more than one answer

Adequacy of directional signs

Question 3

On this visit, were the signs directing your personal group to and within Yellowstone NP adequate?

a. Signs on interstates

Results
- 64% of visitor groups reported directional signs on interstates were adequate (see Figure 30).

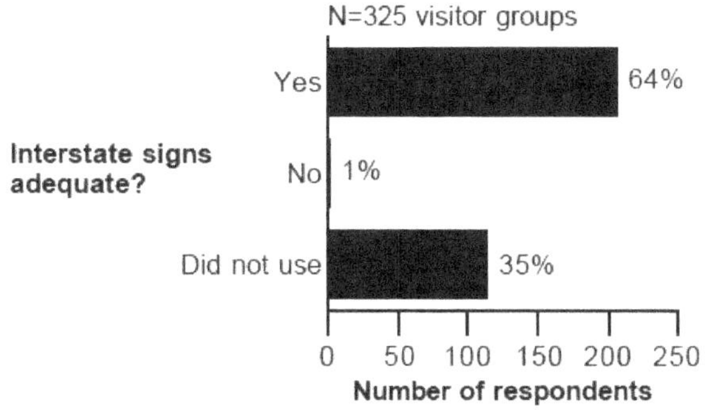

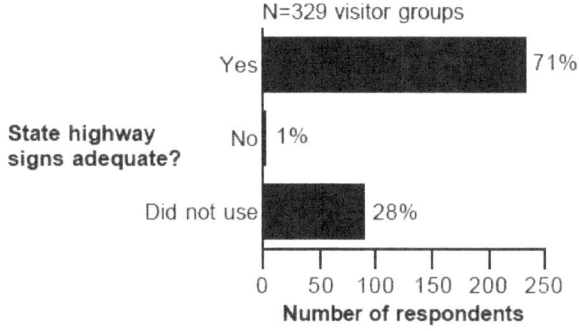

Figure 30. Adequacy of interstate signs

b. Signs on state highways

Results
- 71% of visitor groups said directional signs on state highways were adequate (see Figure 31).

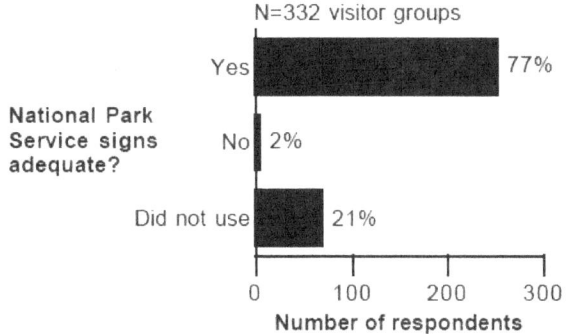

Figure 31. Adequacy of state highway signs

c. National Park Service signs in developed areas of the park

Results
- 77% of visitor groups reported directional signs in developed areas of the park were adequate (see Figure 32).

Figure 32. Adequacy of signs within Yellowstone NP

*total percentages do not equal 100 due to rounding

**total percentages do not equal 100 because visitors could select more than one answer

Number of vehicles used

Question 5c

On this visit, how many vehicles did your personal group use to arrive at the park?

Results

- 81% of visitor groups used one vehicle to arrive at the park (see Figure 33).

- 8% did not use a vehicle.

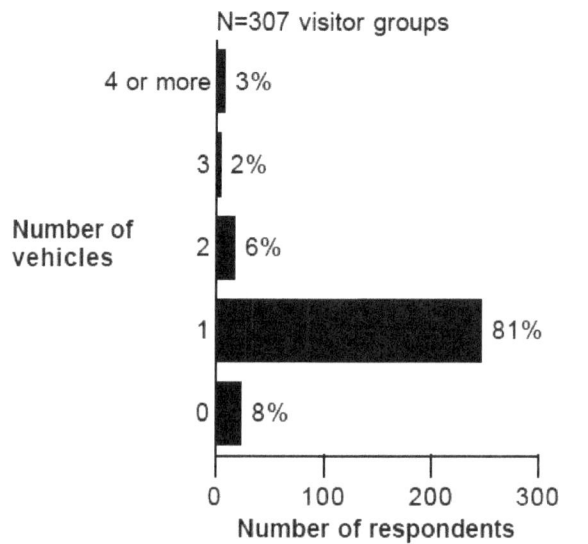

Figure 33. Number of vehicles used to enter the park

Number of park entries

Question 5a

On this visit, how many times did your personal group enter Yellowstone NP during your stay in the area (within 150 miles of the park)?

Results

- 70% of visitor groups entered the park one time (see Figure 34).

- 18% entered twice.

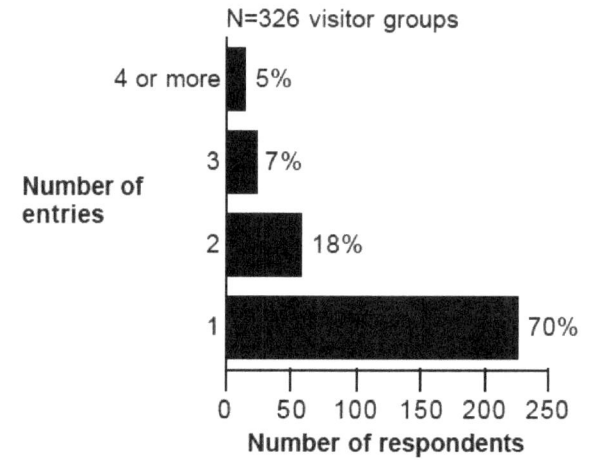

Figure 34. Number of park entries

---

*total percentages do not equal 100 due to rounding
**total percentages do not equal 100 because visitors could select more than one answer

Park entrances used

Question 5b

Which entrances did your personal group use to enter the park?

Results

- 52% of visitor groups entered the park through the West Entrance (see Figure 35).

- 35% used the North Entrance.

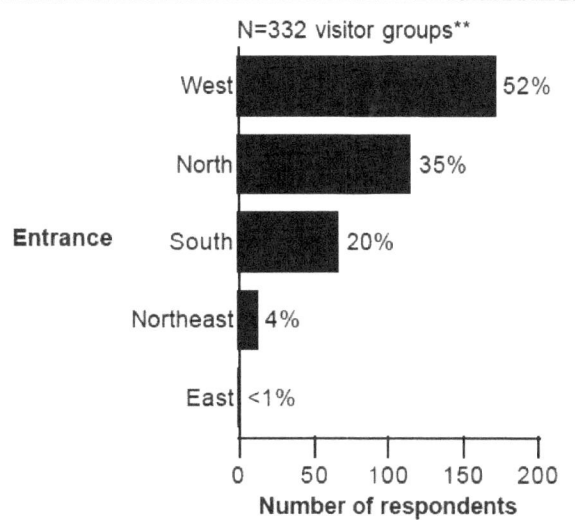

Figure 35. Entrances used to enter the park

Overnight stays

Question 7a

On this trip, did your personal group stay overnight away from home in Yellowstone NP or in the area within 150 miles of the park?

Results

- 85% of visitor groups stayed overnight away from home in the park or in the area within 150 miles of the park (see Figure 36).

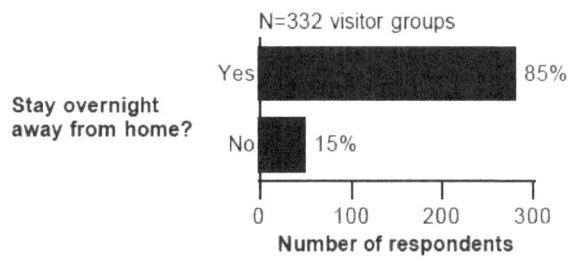

Figure 36. Visitor groups that stayed overnight in the park or within 150 miles of the park

Question 7b

If YES, please list the number of nights your personal group stayed inside the park.

Results

- 29% of visitor groups stayed five or more nights inside Yellowstone NP (see Figure 37).

- 28% stayed two nights.

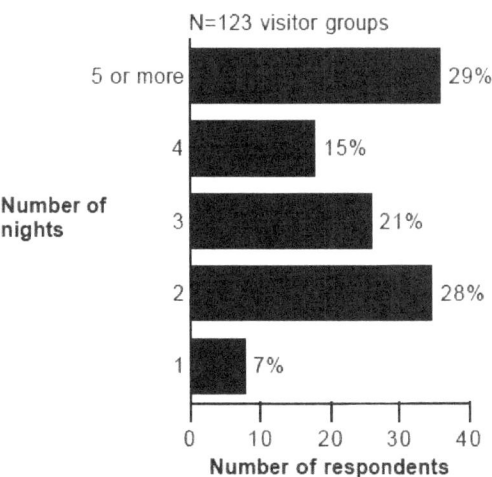

Figure 37. Number of nights spent inside the park

---

*total percentages do not equal 100 due to rounding

**total percentages do not equal 100 because visitors could select more than one answer

Question 7b

If YES, please list the number of nights your personal group stayed outside Yellowstone NP (within 150 miles of the park).

Results

- 37% of visitor groups stayed two or three nights outside the park within 150 miles (see Figure 38).

- 21% stayed six or more nights.

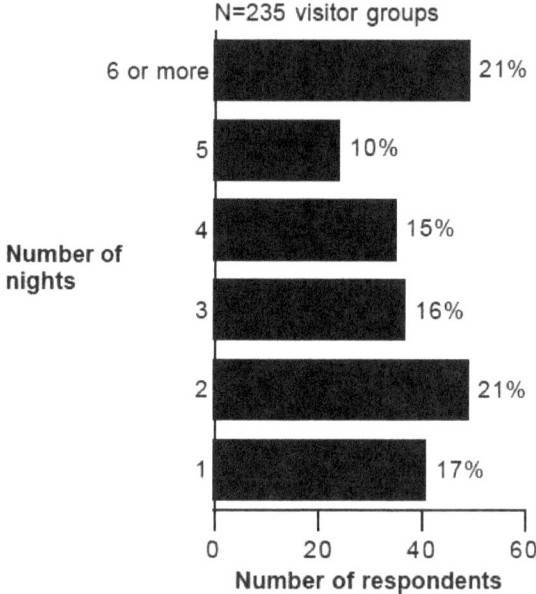

Figure 38. Number of nights spent in the area outside the park (within 150 miles of the park)

Old Faithful Snow Lodge

Question 9a

On this visit, did your personal group visit the Old Faithful Snow Lodge?

Results

- 59% of visitor groups visited the Old Faithful Snow Lodge on this visit (see Figure 39).

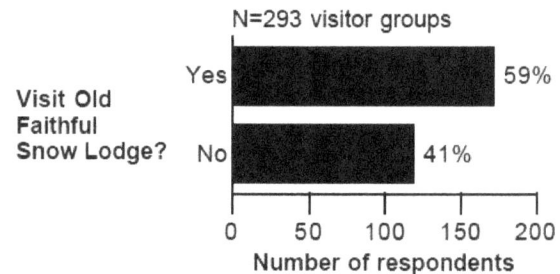

Figure 39. Visitor groups that visited the Old Faithful Snow Lodge

Question 9b

On this visit, did your personal group stay overnight at the Old Faithful Snow Lodge?

Results

- 32% of visitor groups stayed overnight at the Old Faithful Snow Lodge on this visit (see Figure 40).

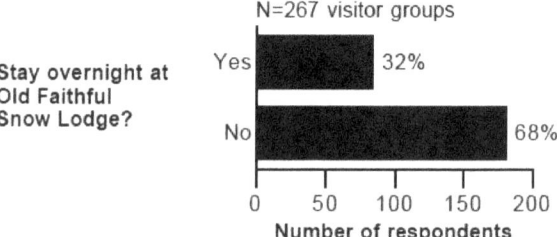

Figure 40. Visitor groups that stayed overnight at the Old Faithful Snow Lodge

*total percentages do not equal 100 due to rounding

**total percentages do not equal 100 because visitors could select more than one answer

Mammoth Hotel

Question 9a

On this visit, did your personal group visit the Mammoth Hotel?

Results

- 35% of visitor groups visited the Mammoth Hotel on this visit (see Figure 41).

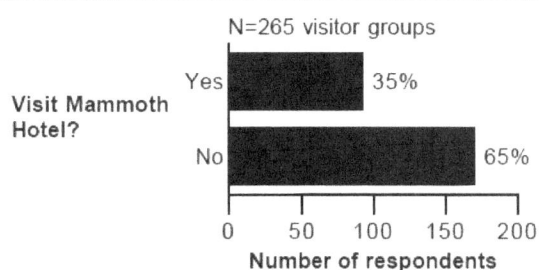

Figure 41. Visitor groups that visited the Mammoth Hotel

Question 9b

On this visit, did your personal group stay overnight at the Mammoth Hotel?

Results

- 31% of visitor groups stayed overnight at the Mammoth Hotel on this visit (see Figure 42).

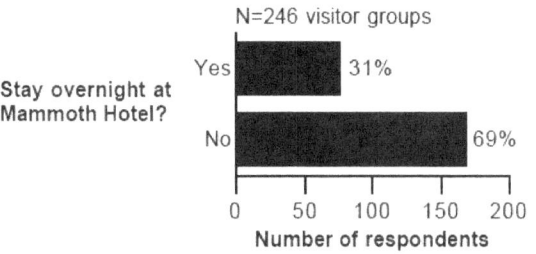

Figure 42. Visitor groups that stayed overnight at the Mammoth Hotel

*total percentages do not equal 100 due to rounding
**total percentages do not equal 100 because visitors could select more than one answer

Accommodations used inside the park

Question 7c

In which types of accommodations did your personal group spend the night(s) inside the park?

Results

- As shown in Figure 43, among those visitor groups that stayed overnight inside the park, the most common types of accommodations used were:

  96% Lodge, motel, cabin, rental condo/home, or bed & breakfast

  3% Residence of friends or relatives

- "Other" type of accommodation (3%) was:

  Yurts

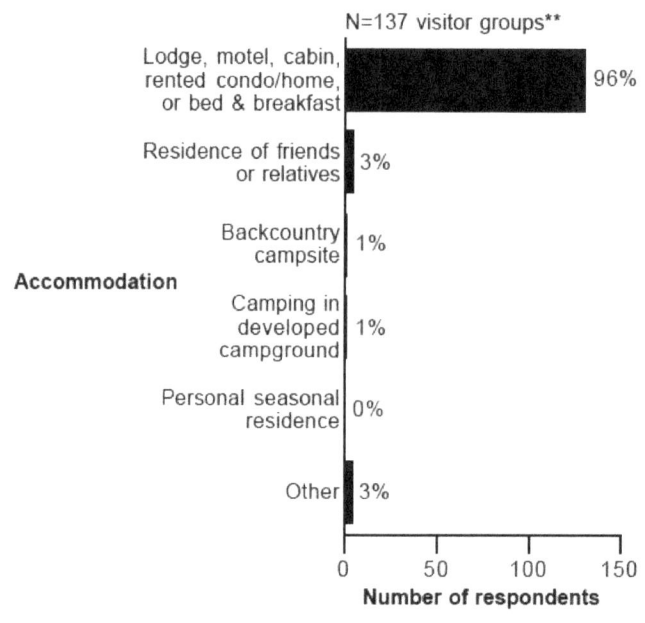

Figure 43. Accommodations used inside the park

Question 7c

If your personal group stayed inside the park, in what type of lodging and at what location did you stay?

Results

- 102 visitor groups listed where they stayed on the night before visiting Yellowstone NP (see Table 14).

Table 14. Accommodations used inside the park
(N=133 comments; some visitor groups made more than one comment)

Location	N	Hotel (%)	Cabin (%)	Yurt (%)
Mammoth Hot Springs	58	98	2	0
Old Faithful	74	81	19	0
Canyon Village – **CAUTION!**	1	0	0	100

*total percentages do not equal 100 due to rounding
**total percentages do not equal 100 because visitors could select more than one answer

Accommodations used outside the park

Question 7d

In which types of accommodations did your personal group spend the night(s) outside park within 150 miles of the park?

Results

- As shown in Figure 44, among those visitor groups that stayed overnight in the area outside the park, the most common types of accommodations used were:

  86% Lodge, hotel, motel, rented condo/home, or bed & breakfast

  6% Residence of friends or relatives

- "Other" types of accommodations (16%) were:

  Camped in vehicle
  Church in Gardiner
  RV

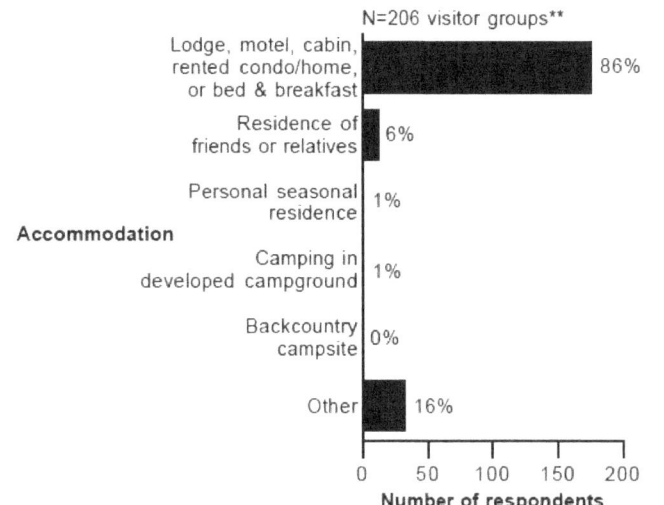

Figure 44. Accommodations used outside the park within 150 miles

---

*total percentages do not equal 100 due to rounding

**total percentages do not equal 100 because visitors could select more than one answer

Places stayed on night prior to visit

Question 8a

On this trip, where did your personal group stay on the night before visiting Yellowstone NP? (Open-ended)

Results

- 317 visitor groups listed where they stayed on the night before visiting Yellowstone NP (see Table 15).

Table 15. Places stayed on the night before arrival at Yellowstone NP (N=67 places)

Place	Number of times mentioned	Percent
West Yellowstone, MT	77	24
Jackson, WY	54	17
Big Sky, MT	33	10
Bozeman, MT	33	10
Billings, MT	12	4
Gardiner, MT	9	3
Helena, MT	8	3
Missoula, MT	6	2
Butte, MT	5	2
Chico Hot Springs, MT	5	2
Buffalo, WY	4	1
Island Park, ID	3	1
Salt Lake City, UT	3	1
Wilson, WY	3	1
Cody, WY	2	1
Dillon, MT	2	1
Emigrant, MT	2	1
Gallatin Gateway, MT	2	1
Lander, WY	2	1
Livingston, MT	2	1
Moose, WY	2	1
Ogden, UT	2	1
Pray, MT	2	1
Atlanta, GA	1	<1
Belgrade, MT	1	<1
Belle Fourche, SD	1	<1
Bellevue, WA	1	<1
Bismarck, ND	1	<1
Blackfoot, ID	1	<1
Boise, ID	1	<1
Boulder, MT	1	<1
Brooklyn, NY	1	<1
Clyde Park, MT	1	<1
Conifer, CO	1	<1

*total percentages do not equal 100 due to rounding

**total percentages do not equal 100 because visitors could select more than one answer

Table 15. Places stayed on the night before arrival at Yellowstone NP (continued)

Place	Number of times mentioned	Percent
Deer Lodge, MT	1	<1
East Helena, MT	1	<1
East Wendover, UT	1	<1
Ennis, MT	1	<1
Ft. Lauderdale, FL	1	<1
Hamilton, MT	1	<1
Hermann, MO	1	<1
Highlands Park, CO	1	<1
Idaho Falls, ID	1	<1
Langhorne, PA	1	<1
Laramie, WY	1	<1
Lees Summit, MO	1	<1
Los Angeles, CA	1	<1
Melbourne, Australia	1	<1
Midvale, UT	1	<1
Moran, WY	1	<1
Napa, CA	1	<1
New York, NY	1	<1
Pocatello, ID	1	<1
Powell, WY	1	<1
Raynesford, MT	1	<1
Rexburg, ID	1	<1
Ringle, WI	1	<1
Roy, UT	1	<1
Seattle, WA	1	<1
Sheridan, WY	1	<1
St. Regis, MT	1	<1
Teton Village, WY	1	<1
Thermopolis, WY	1	<1
Togwotee Mtn Lodge, WY	1	<1
Town north of West Entrance	1	<1
Victor, ID	1	<1
Winter Park, FL	1	<1

*total percentages do not equal 100 due to rounding
**total percentages do not equal 100 because visitors could select more than one answer

Places stayed on night after visit

Question 8b

On this trip, where did your personal group stay on the night after visiting Yellowstone NP? (Open-ended)

Results

- 313 visitor groups listed the places they stayed on the night after visiting Yellowstone NP (see Table 16).

Table 16. Places stayed on the night after visiting Yellowstone NP (N=76 places)

Place	Number of times mentioned	Percent
West Yellowstone, MT	58	19
Jackson, WY	51	16
Big Sky, MT	38	12
Bozeman, MT	34	11
Helena, MT	10	3
Billings, MT	7	2
Gardiner, MT	6	2
Missoula, MT	6	2
Salt Lake City, UT	6	2
Butte, MT	5	2
Chico Hot Springs, MT	4	1
Sheridan, WY	4	1
Island Park, ID	3	1
Lander, WY	3	1
Ogden, UT	3	1
Wilson, WY	3	1
Casper, WY	2	1
Cheyenne, WY	2	1
Cody, WY	2	1
Emigrant, MT	2	1
Idaho Falls, ID	2	1
Laramie, WY	2	1
Livingston, MT	2	1
Moose, WY	2	1
Moran, WY	2	1
Spokane, WA	2	1
Twin Falls, ID	2	1
Atlanta, GA	1	<1
Belgrade, MT	1	<1
Belle Fourche, SD	1	<1
Bismarck, ND	1	<1
Blackfoot, ID	1	<1
Bloomington, ID	1	<1
Boise, ID	1	<1

*total percentages do not equal 100 due to rounding

**total percentages do not equal 100 because visitors could select more than one answer

Table 16. Places stayed on the night after visiting at Yellowstone NP (continued)

Place	Number of times mentioned	Percent
Boulder, MT	1	<1
Brooklyn, NY	1	<1
Buffalo, WY	1	<1
Cedar City, UT	1	<1
Clyde Park, MT	1	<1
Conifer, CO	1	<1
Dayton, OH	1	<1
Denver, CO	1	<1
Dillon, MT	1	<1
East Helena, MT	1	<1
Ennis, MT	1	<1
Farmington, UT	1	<1
Ft. Collins, CO	1	<1
Ft. Lauderdale, FL	1	<1
Gallatin Gateway, MT	1	<1
Gloversville, NY	1	<1
Goodyear, AZ	1	<1
Great Falls, MT	1	<1
Hamilton, MT	1	<1
Hermann, MO	1	<1
Highlands Park, CO	1	<1
Kalispell, MT	1	<1
La Grande, OR	1	<1
Lees Summit, MO	1	<1
Los Angeles, CA	1	<1
Midvale, UT	1	<1
Napa, CA	1	<1
New York, NY	1	<1
Parker, CO	1	<1
Polson, MT	1	<1
Powell, WY	1	<1
Provo, UT	1	<1
Rawlins, WY	1	<1
Raynesford, MT	1	<1
Rexburg, ID	1	<1
Ritzville, WA	1	<1
Roy, UT	1	<1
Teton Village, WY	1	<1
Thermopolis, WY	1	<1
Town southeast of Grand Teton, WY	1	<1
Victor, ID	1	<1
Wheatland, WY	1	<1

*total percentages do not equal 100 due to rounding
**total percentages do not equal 100 because visitors could select more than one answer

Total length of visit

Question 6
For this trip, please list the total time your personal group spent in Yellowstone NP.

Number of hours if less than 24

Results
- 75% of visitor groups stayed 6 - 10 hours in the park (see Figure 45).

- 16% spent up to five hours in the park.

- 6% spent 16 or more hours in the park.

- The average length of stay for visitor groups that spent less than 24 hours was 7.7 hours.

Number of days if 24 hours or more

- 31% of visitor groups spent three days in the park (see Figure 46).

- 20% spent six or more days in the park.

- 19% spent two days in the park.

- The average length of stay for visitor groups that spent 24 hours or more was 3.8 days.

Average length of stay for all visitors

- The average length of stay for all visitor groups was 45.6 hours, or 2 days.

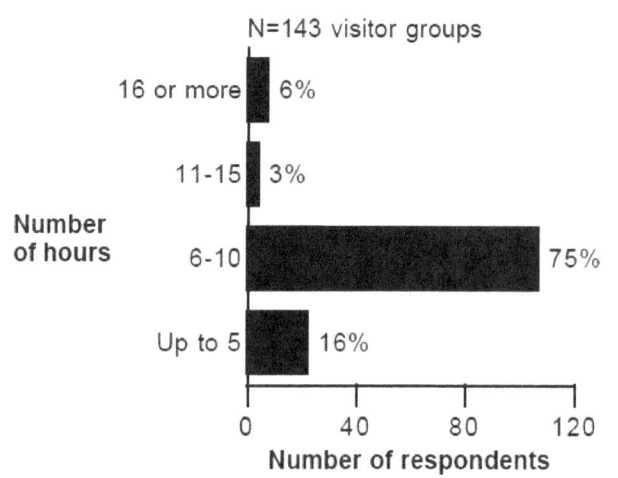

Figure 45. Number of hours spent in the park

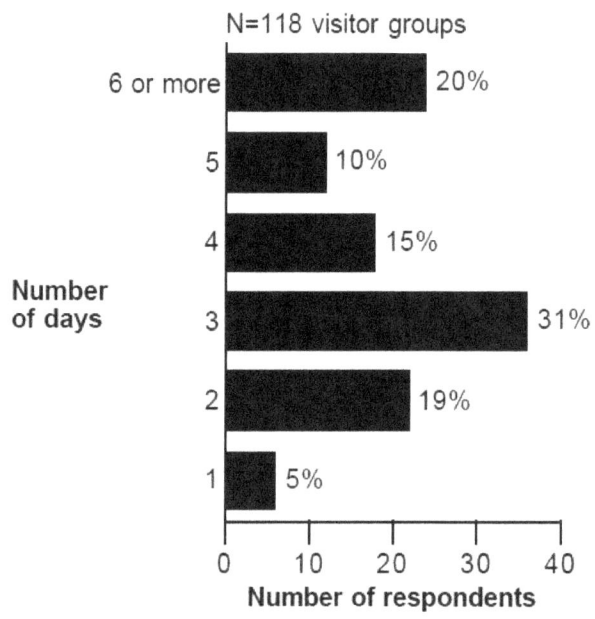

Figure 46. Number of days spent in the park

*total percentages do not equal 100 due to rounding
**total percentages do not equal 100 because visitors could select more than one answer

Locations visited

Question 6d

Was your personal group able to visit all the locations in Yellowstone NP that you had planned to visit?

Results
- 88% of visitor groups were able to visit all the locations they had planned to visit on this trip (see Figure 47).

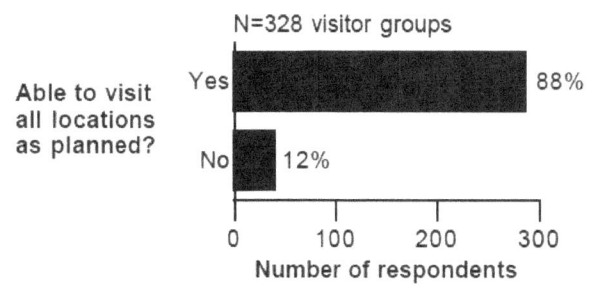

Figure 47. Visitor groups that were able to visit all locations as planned

Question 6a

For this trip, please indicate all the park locations that your personal group visited in Yellowstone NP.

Results
- As shown in Figure 48, the most common locations visited by visitor groups were:

  79% Old Faithful
  41% Madison
  38% Mammoth Hot Springs

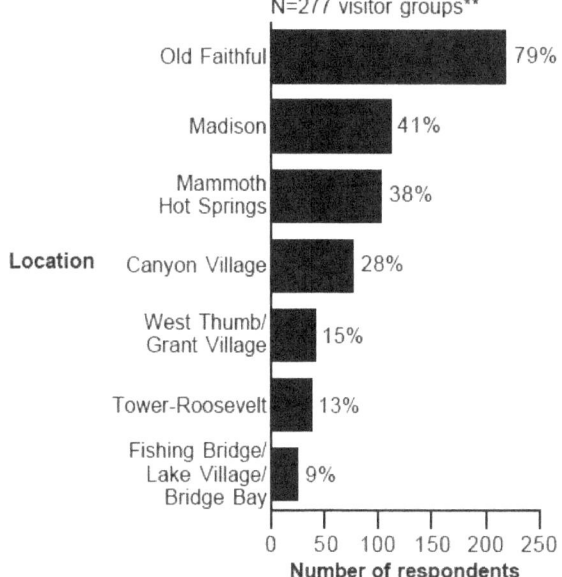

Figure 48. Locations visited in the park

---

*total percentages do not equal 100 due to rounding
**total percentages do not equal 100 because visitors could select more than one answer

Reasons for not visiting locations in the park

Question 6e

If you were not able to visit all the locations in the park you planned, why not? (Open-ended)

Results

- 38 visitor groups responded to this question.

- Table 17 lists visitor groups' reasons for not visiting park locations.

Table 17. Reasons visitor groups were unable to visit selected locations within the park (N=43 comments; some visitor groups made more than one comment.)

Reason	Number of comments
Weather conditions	11
Not enough time	6
Snowcoach tour route	5
Road closures	3
Took a guided snowmobile trip	3
Snowcoach broke down	2
Bad planning by snowcoach drivers	1
Closed for winter	1
Could not do multiple tours	1
Cross country ski shuttle was sold out	1
Didn't have right kind of vehicle for roads	1
Group too big	1
Lack of snow transport to area at time of day	1
Personal snowmobiles not allowed	1
Ski drops were not very flexible	1
Snowcoach problems	1
Too far for a day visit	1
Vehicle breakdown	1
Winter hours	1

*total percentages do not equal 100 due to rounding

**total percentages do not equal 100 because visitors could select more than one answer

Locations not visited in the park

Question 6f

Which locations were your personal group unable to visit?
(Open-ended)

Results – Interpret results with **CAUTION!**

- 28 visitor groups responded to this question.

- The locations that visitor groups were unable to visit are listed in Table 18.

Table 18. Locations in park that visitor groups were unable to visit on this trip (N=49 comments; some visitor groups made more than one comment.) – **CAUTION!**

Location	Number of times mentioned
Mammoth Hot Springs	8
Tower-Roosevelt	5
Canyon Village	3
Norris	3
Old Faithful	3
West Thumb	3
Hayden Valley	2
Madison	2
Biscuit Basin	1
Black Sand "Thumper"	1
Canyons and dragons mouth	1
East side of lower loop	1
Everything except Canyon Village, Old Faithful	1
Everything except Mammoth Hot Springs and Tower-Roosevelt	1
Everything except road from Gardiner to Cooke City	1
Firehole Lake Drive	1
Fishing Bridge	1
Lake Village	1
Lamar Valley	1
Mammoth	1
Mammoth and drivers	1
Many due to winter	1
Paint pots	1
Snow Lodge	1
The main lodge	1
Tower ski trail	1
Yellowstone Lake	1
Yellowstone River	1

---

*total percentages do not equal 100 due to rounding

**total percentages do not equal 100 because visitors could select more than one answer

Number of hours spent at selected park locations

Question 6b
Please list the amount of time you spent at each location (hours spent – if less than 24 hours).

Results
- The time spent at selected park locations is shown in Table 19.

- At each location, the most common length of visit was between one and two hours.

- The highest average number of hours spent was five hours, at Mammoth Hot Springs.

Table 19. Number of hours spent at each park location
(N=number of visitor groups)

Location	N	Mean	Less than 1 hour	1-2 hours	3-4 hours	5 or more hours
			Time spent (%)*			
Mammoth Hot Springs	37	5	3	45	24	27
Madison	108	1	7	83	5	5
Old Faithful	141	2	1	72	20	7
West Thumb/Grant Village	38	1	3	95	3	0
Fishing Bridge/Lake Village/Bridge Bay – **CAUTION!**	25	1	8	92	0	0
Tower-Roosevelt	40	3	5	45	28	23
Canyon Village	79	2	4	76	14	6

Number of days spent at selected park locations

Question 6c
Please list the amount of time you spent at each location (days spent – if more than 24 hours).

Results
- The time spent at selected park locations is shown in Table 20.

- Mammoth Hot Springs and Old Faithful had the highest number of overnight visitors.

Table 20. Number of days spent at each park location
(N=number of visitor groups)

Location	N	Mean	1 day	2 days	3 days	4 or more days
			Time spent (%)*			
Mammoth Hot Springs	76	3	21	30	30	18
Madison – **CAUTION!**	3	2	67	0	0	33
Old Faithful	83	3	11	33	33	24
West Thumb/Grant Village – **CAUTION!**	2	2	50	0	50	0
Fishing Bridge/Lake Village/Bridge Bay – **CAUTION!**	0	0	0	0	0	0
Tower-Roosevelt – **CAUTION!**	3	2	33	33	0	33
Canyon Village – **CAUTION!**	3	3	33	0	0	67

*total percentages do not equal 100 due to rounding
**total percentages do not equal 100 because visitors could select more than one answer

Activities on this visit

Question 11a

On this visit, in which activities did your personal group participate within Yellowstone NP?

Results

- As shown in Figure 49, the most common activities in which visitor groups participated on this visit were:

    86% Viewing wildlife/ birdwatching
    77% Boardwalk/geyser basin
    66% Eating in park restaurants
    63% Snowcoach tour

- Other activities (32%) were:

    Boiling River
    Dogsledding
    Hiking
    Ice skating
    Junior Ranger activities
    Meeting new people
    Meeting with park staff at the Yellowstone Center for Resources
    Old Faithful viewing
    Outdoor winter activity
    See Yellowstone in winter
    Visiting Lamar Basin Ranch
    Winter Wonderland Tour
    Wolf Discovery Tour
    Yellowstone Association/ Institute lodging and learning program
    Yurt Camp at Canyon Village

Note: Data for snowmobiling was compiled from "other" open-ended responses.

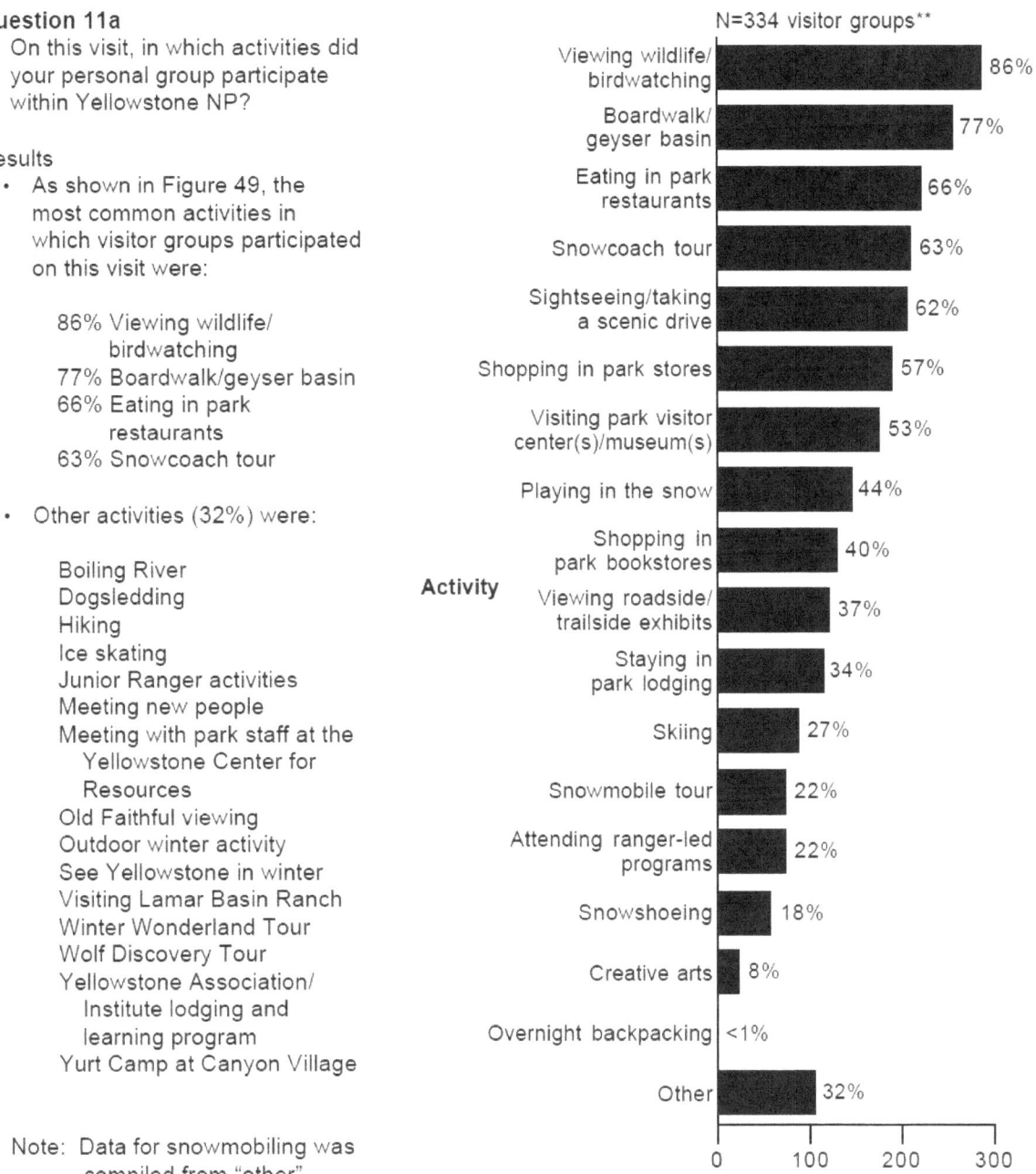

Figure 49. Activities on this visit

---

*total percentages do not equal 100 due to rounding
**total percentages do not equal 100 because visitors could select more than one answer

Question 11a

On this visit, how many park visitor centers/ museums did you and your personal group visit within Yellowstone NP?

Results

- 69% of visitor groups visited one park visitor center/museum (see Figure 50).

- 28% visited two visitor centers/museums.

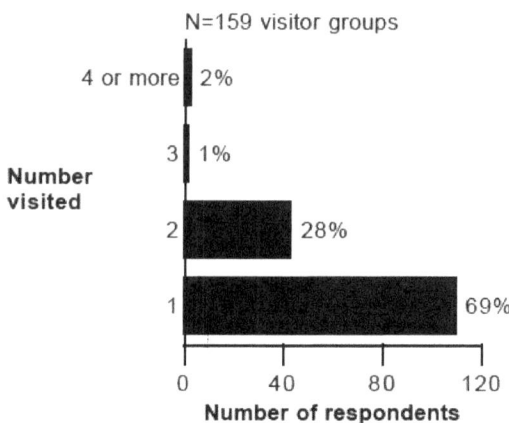

Figure 50. Number of visitor centers/museums visited

---

*total percentages do not equal 100 due to rounding

**total percentages do not equal 100 because visitors could select more than one answer

Activity that was primary reason for visiting Yellowstone NP

Question 11b

Which one of the above activities was the primary reason your personal group visited Yellowstone NP on this visit? (Open ended)

Results

- As shown in Figure 51, the most common activities listed as visitor groups' primary reason for visiting the park were:

    26% Snowcoach tour
    23% Snowmobile tour
    17% Viewing wildlife/ birdwatching

Note: Data for snowmobiling was compiled from "other" openended responses.

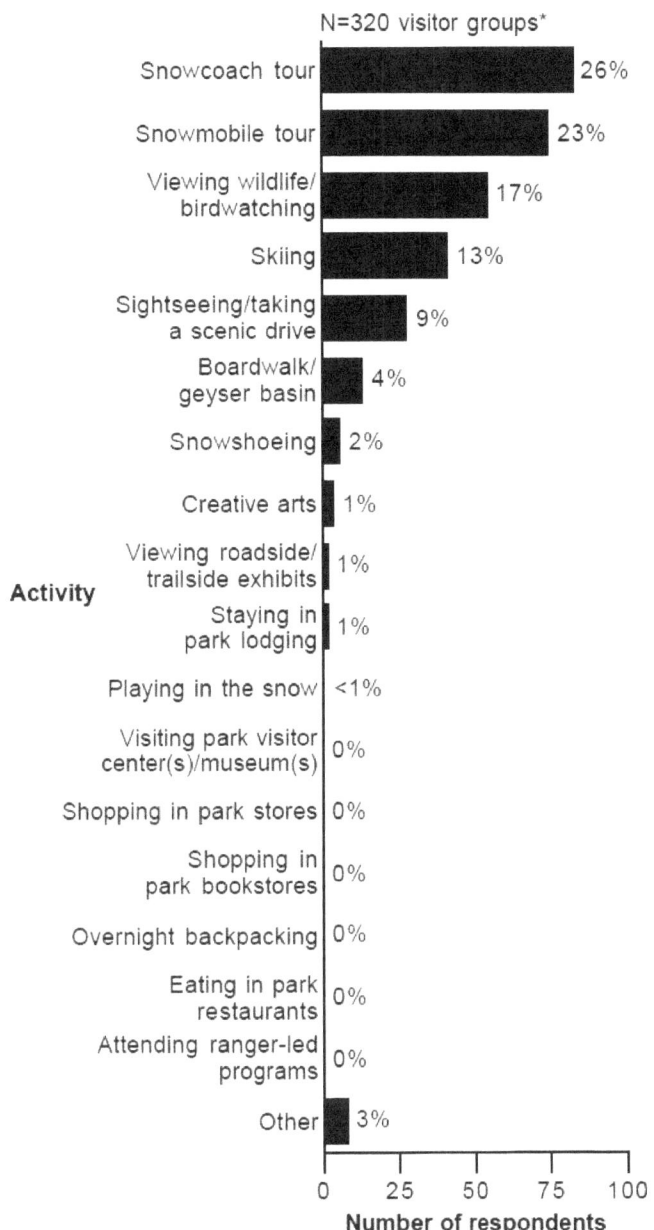

Figure 51. Activity that was primary reason for visiting Yellowstone NP

*total percentages do not equal 100 due to rounding

**total percentages do not equal 100 because visitors could select more than one answer

Ratings of Concession Services and Activities

Locating commercial services

Question 4a

In Yellowstone NP, did your personal group have any problem finding commercial services (such as lodging, food, gas, gift shops, etc.)?

Results

- 3% of visitor groups had difficulty finding commercial services on this trip (see Figure 52).

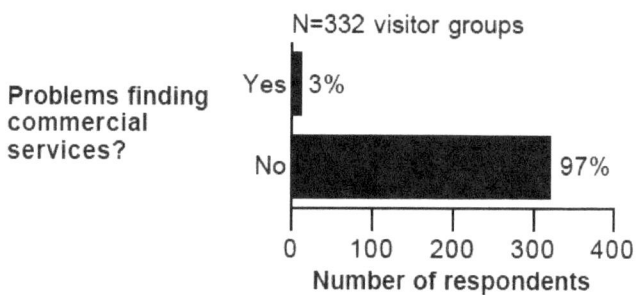

Figure 52. Visitor groups that had problems finding commercial services

Question 4b

If YES, which of the following reasons contributed to the problem?

Results – Interpret results with **CAUTION!**

- Not enough visitor groups responded to this question to provide reliable results (see Figure 53).

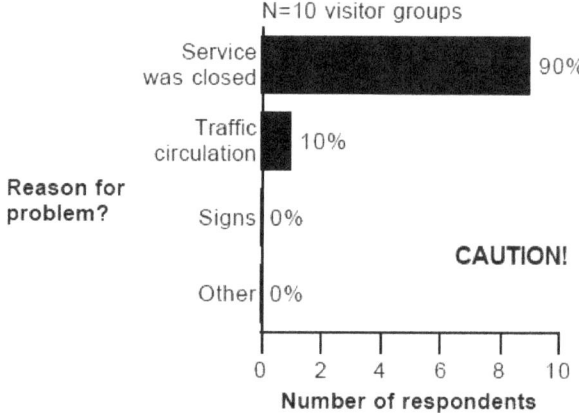

Figure 53. Reasons for difficulty locating commercial services

---

*total percentages do not equal 100 due to rounding

**total percentages do not equal 100 because visitors could select more than one answer

Commercial services used in Yellowstone NP

Question 13a

On this visit to Yellowstone NP, which of
the following commercial services did
your personal group use?

Results

- As shown in Figure 54, the most
  commonly used commercial services
  by visitor groups were:

  71% Restaurants/food service
  55% Snowcoach tour
  50% Lodging

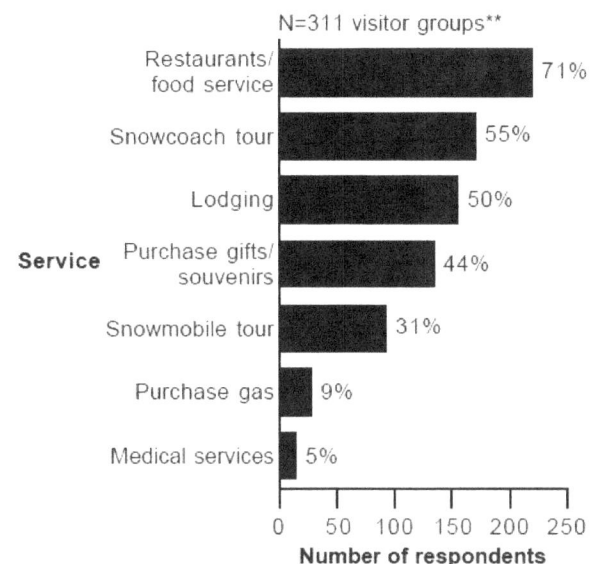

Figure 54. Commercial services used

---

*total percentages do not equal 100 due to rounding
**total percentages do not equal 100 because visitors could select more than one answer

Question 13b

If your personal group used lodging, campgrounds and/or restaurants/food services, were you able to get your first choice of location?

Results

- As shown in Table 21, visitor groups were able to get their first choice of location for the following services:

    96% Restaurants/food service
    92% Lodging

Question 13c

Did the commercial services that your personal group used meet your expectations?

Results

- As shown in Table 21, the services that exceeded visitor expectations included:

    66% Snowcoach tour
    65% Snowmobile tour
    40% Lodging

Table 21. Ability to get first choice of commercial services and whether the services met expectations (N=number of visitor groups)

Service	b) **Able to get first choice? (%)**			c) **Did commercial service meet expectations? Rating (%)***			
	N	Yes	No	N	Worse than expected	About what was expected	Better than expected
Lodging	133	92	8	141	4	56	40
Restaurants/food service	214	96	4	236	8	53	39
Purchase gas – **CAUTION!**	n/a	n/a	n/a	16	0	81	19
Purchase gifts/ souvenirs	n/a	n/a	n/a	146	4	67	29
Medical services – **CAUTION!**	n/a	n/a	n/a	2	0	50	50
Snowcoach tour	n/a	n/a	n/a	195	3	31	66
Snowmobile tour	n/a	n/a	n/a	89	6	29	65

*total percentages do not equal 100 due to rounding
**total percentages do not equal 100 because visitors could select more than one answer

Explanation of any "no" and "worse than expected" responses

Question 13e

If you marked "No" or "Worse than expected" to part (b) or (c) of this question, please explain where and why.

Results

- 59 visitor groups responded to this question.

- Table 22 shows the categories, locations, and comments made by visitor groups who didn't get their first choice and/or whose expectations weren't met.

- 21% of the comments were about the poor quality of food served.

- 11% of the comments mentioned a need for more variety in the menu options related to price, health food, ethnic options, kids foods, and general variety.

Table 22. Explanations of "no" and "worse than expected" responses to choices and expectations for commercial services
(N=61 comments; some visitor groups made more than one comment.)

Location	Comment	Number of times mentioned
Lodging		
Mammoth Hot Springs Hotel	Room far too hot	2
Mammoth Hot Springs Hotel	Small rooms and uncomfortable	2
Old Faithful cabin	Very uncomfortable beds	2
No specific location provided	Could not get lodging inside the park	1
No specific location provided	Need better lodging options in winter	1
Madison	Warming hut	1
Mammoth Hot Springs Hotel	Wanted room with one queen	1
Old Faithful Frontier cabin	Dirty, leaky doors, linens didn't fit	1
Old Faithful Frontier cabin	Frontier full so stayed in Western cabin	1
Restaurants/food service		
Old Faithful restaurant	Food was poor quality	5
Mammoth Hotel Dining Room	Food was poor quality	4
Old Faithful Snow Lodge	Not enough menu options	3
Geyser Grill	Food was poor quality	2
Old Faithful Restaurant	Service too slow	2
Old Faithful Snow Lodge	Food was poor quality	2
No specific location provided	Crowded, limited seating, felt rushed	1
No specific location provided	Not enough menu options	1
No specific location provided	Overpriced food	1
Geyser Grill	Out of hot cider	1
Geyser Grill	Overpriced food	1
Mammoth Hotel Dining Room	Overpriced food	1
Mammoth Hotel Dining Room	Service was slow and bad	1
Old Faithful Restaurant	Closed	1
Old Faithful Restaurant	Would like to have more ethnic choices	1

*total percentages do not equal 100 due to rounding
**total percentages do not equal 100 because visitors could select more than one answer

Table 22. Explanations of "no" and "worse than expected" responses to choices and expectations for commercial services (continued)

Location	Comment	Number of times mentioned
Restaurants/food service (continued)		
Old Faithful Snow Lodge	Menu choices were too fancy	1
Old Faithful Snow Lodge	Overpriced food	1
Old Faithful Snow Lodge	Service varied from good to bad	1
Restaurant in Old Faithful Lodge	Not a great menu for kids	1
Restaurant in Old Faithful Lodge	Overpriced food	1
Shops		
Mammoth Hot Springs	Need more variety of goods	2
Gift shop in Snow Lodge	Low quality gift items	1
Gift shop in Snow Lodge	Very touristy	1
Old Faithful	Low quality gift items	1
Old Faithful	Need more variety of goods	1
Concessions		
Snowmobile trails	Roads/trails poorly groomed - dangerous	2
Tours - general	Didn't see much at all	2
Ski and snowshoe rental shops	Some personnel were not trained	1
Snowcoach tour	Limited sightseeing/too much travel time	1
Snowcoach tour	Overpriced	1
Snowmobile tour	More instruction for operating safely	1
Snowmobile trails	Much more demanding than expected	1
Tours - general	Couldn't get tour in park, used other company services	1
Tours - general	Tour went too fast	1

*total percentages do not equal 100 due to rounding

**total percentages do not equal 100 because visitors could select more than one answer

Value of commercial services for money paid

Question 13d

Please rate (from 1 to 5) the value of the commercial services your personal group used, for the money you paid.

Results

- As shown in Figure 55, the commercial services that received the highest combined "very good" and "good" ratings of value for money paid were:

  77% Snowcoach tour
  75% Snowmobile tour
  74% Lodging

- Table 23 shows the ratings of each service for money paid.

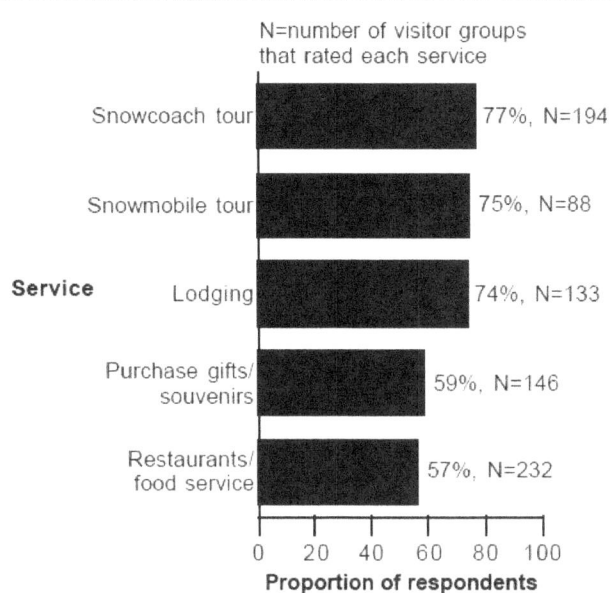

N=number of visitor groups that rated each service

Figure 55. Combined proportions of "very good" and "good" ratings of value of commercial services for money paid

Table 23. Ratings of value of commercial services for money paid (N=number of visitor groups)

Service	N	Very poor	Poor	Average	Good	Very good
		Rating (%)*				
Lodging	133	0	4	23	48	26
Restaurants/food service	232	1	8	34	34	23
Purchase gas – **CAUTION!**	16	0	0	81	6	13
Purchase gifts/souvenirs	146	0	1	40	45	14
Medical services – **CAUTION!**	1	0	0	0	0	100
Snowcoach tour	194	0	6	17	31	46
Snowmobile tour	88	1	3	20	32	43

*total percentages do not equal 100 due to rounding
**total percentages do not equal 100 because visitors could select more than one answer

Explanation of "very poor" or "poor" ratings of value of commercial services for money paid

Question 13f

If you marked "very poor" or "poor" in part (d) of this question please explain where and why.

Results – Interpret results with **CAUTION!**

- 29 visitor groups responded to this question.

- Table 24 shows the categories, locations and comments made by visitor groups that rated the value of commercial services as either "very poor" or "poor" for money paid.

- 40% of all comments were critical of the prices being too high.

Table 24. Explanations of "very poor" or "poor" ratings of commercial services for money paid (N=33 comments; some visitor groups made more than one comment.) – **CAUTION!**

Location	Comment	Number of times mentioned
Lodging		
Mammoth Hot Springs Hotel	Couldn't sleep	1
Old Faithful Frontier cabin	Cabins need maintenance	1
Old Faithful Snow Lodge	Too expensive	1
Old Faithful cabin	Leaky sink and snow came in under door	1
Old Faithful cabin	Very uncomfortable beds	1
Shops		
No location specified	Prices too high for what you get	1
Restaurants/food service		
Mammoth Hotel Dining Room	Food quality and taste not acceptable	2
Mammoth Hotel Dining Room	Prices too high	2
Old Faithful Snow Lodge Restaurant	Poor quality food	2
Geyser Grill	Food was bad	1
Geyser Grill	Prices too high	1
Mammoth Hotel Dining Room	Limited selection of items	1
No location specified	Overpriced	1
Old Faithful Snow Lodge Restaurant	Food was very bad	1
Old Faithful Snow Lodge Restaurant	Limited selection of items	1
Concessions		
Snowcoach tour	Too expensive	5
Snowmobile tour	Tour went too fast	2
Snowcoach tour	Tour went too fast	1
Snowmobile tour	Should provide alternative in bad weather	1
Snowmobile tour	Too expensive	1
Snowmobile trails	Poorly groomed and dangerous	1

*total percentages do not equal 100 due to rounding

**total percentages do not equal 100 because visitors could select more than one answer

Table 24. Explanations of "very poor" or "poor" ratings of commercial services for money paid (continued)

Location	Comment	Number of times mentioned
General		
Mammoth (unspecified)	Too expensive	2
No location specified	Choices were limited	1
No location specified	Guide didn't have enough knowledge of the park	1

---

*total percentages do not equal 100 due to rounding

**total percentages do not equal 100 because visitors could select more than one answer

Explanation of "very good" ratings of value of commercial services for money paid

Question 13g
If you marked "very good" in part (d) of this question, please explain.

Results
- 120 visitor groups responded to this question.

- Table 25 shows comments made by visitor groups that rated the value of commercial services as "very good" for money paid.

Table 25. Explanation of "very good" ratings of value of commercial services for money paid (N=170 comments; some visitor groups made more than one comment.)

Comment	Number of times mentioned
Lodging	
Comfortable rooms/beds	5
Cabins were nice/great value	2
Lodging was excellent	2
Snow Lodge was awesome	2
Snow Lodge was clean and comfortable	2
Great value for the price at Mammoth	1
Historic atmosphere was great	1
Mammoth Hot Springs Hotel was excellent	1
Nice rooms	1
Yurts were outstanding accommodations	1
Restaurants/food service	
Good/excellent food and service	26
Reasonable prices	5
Mammoth restaurant was very good	3
Good selection	1
Snow Lodge food was great	1
Concessions	
Great/excellent tour guide	54
Snowcoach tour was amazing	13
Tour was great	10
Comfortable snowcoach	4
Good equipment	3
Snowmobile guide/tour was excellent	3
Great value for the price	1
Love coming for snowmobiling	1
Reasonable prices	1
Yellowstone Association tour had excellent guides	1

---

*total percentages do not equal 100 due to rounding
**total percentages do not equal 100 because visitors could select more than one answer

Table 25. Explanation of "very good" ratings of value of commercial services for money paid (continued)

Comment	Number of times mentioned
Shops	
Reasonable prices	3
Enjoyed the shop atmosphere	1
Service at gift/ski shop was great	1
Shops were great	1
General	
Reasonable prices	7
The atmosphere was wonderful	3
Friendly staff	2
Love coming to park numerous times a year	2
Visiting park is priceless experience	2
Great time with friends	1
Park was very nice and clean	1
Saw lots of wildlife	1

*total percentages do not equal 100 due to rounding
**total percentages do not equal 100 because visitors could select more than one answer

Planned/reserved concession services and activities

Question 14a

Prior to your visit to Yellowstone NP, which concession services and activities did your personal group plan to do, or make reservations for, before arrival?

Results

- As shown in Figure 56, the most common concession services and activities that were planned or reserved before arrival were:

  65% Snowcoach tour
  35% Snowmobile tour

- The concession service/activity least planned for was:

  4% Yellowstone Association Institute class

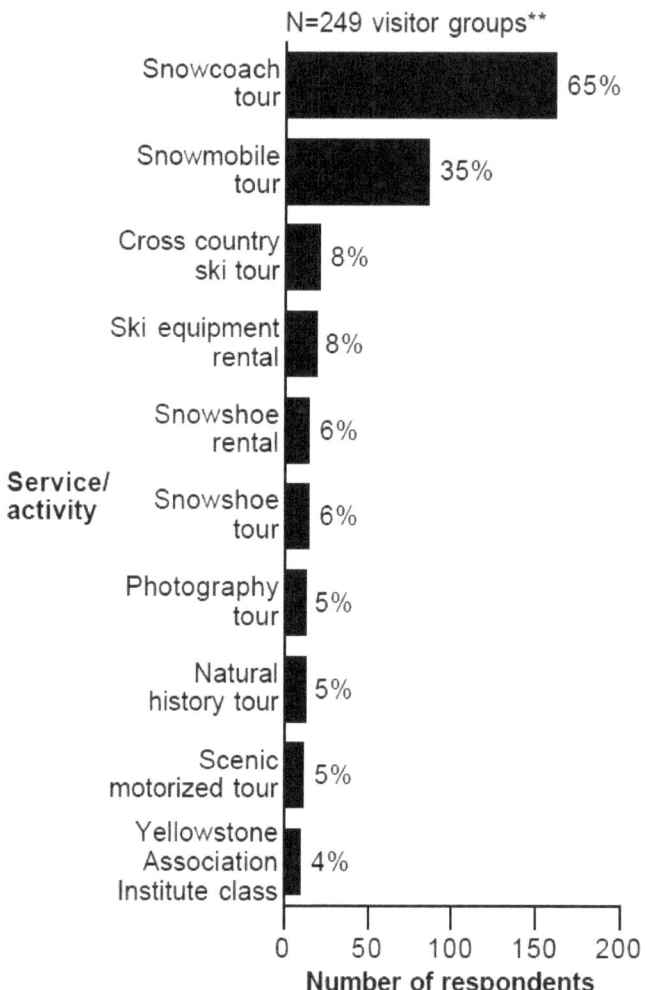

Figure 56. Concession services or activities planned or reserved before arrival

---

*total percentages do not equal 100 due to rounding

**total percentages do not equal 100 because visitors could select more than one answer

Concession services and activities used

Question 14b

Please indicate all the concession services and activities that your personal group used during this visit to Yellowstone NP.

Results

- As shown in Figure 57, the most common concession services and activities used by visitor groups were:

  62% Snowcoach tour
  32% Snowmobile tour

- The least used concession service/ activity was:

  4% Yellowstone Association Institute class

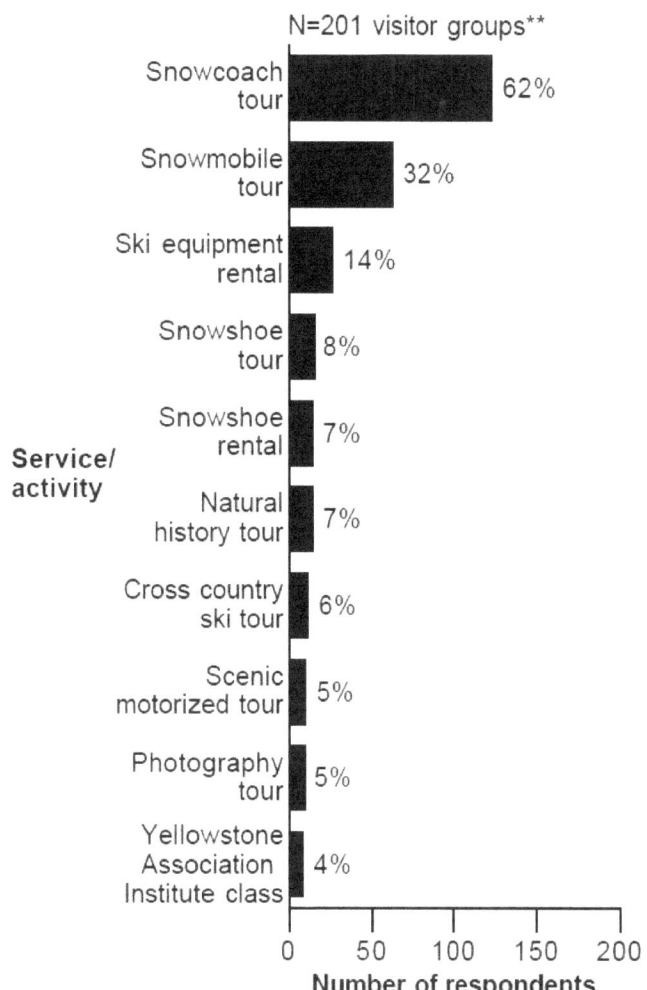

N=201 visitor groups**

Figure 57. Concession services or activities used

*total percentages do not equal 100 due to rounding

**total percentages do not equal 100 because visitors could select more than one answer

Comparison of concession services and activities planned/reserved vs. used

Question 14

a. Prior to your visit to Yellowstone NP, which concession services and activities did your personal group plan to do, or make reservations for, before arrival?

b. Please indicate all the concession services and activities that your personal group used during this visit to Yellowstone NP.

Note: The N for Figure 56 and the N for Table 26 do not match due to inconsistencies in responses to this question.

Results

- Table 26 shows the reported success rates of visitor groups that planned activities and completed those activities.

- Results for activities planned/completed by N<30 visitor groups may be unreliable.

- The activities most often completed by visitor groups were:

  95% Snowcoach tour
  93% Snowshoe tour

Table 26. Success rates of visitor groups that planned an activity and completed it as planned (N=number of visitor groups)

Activity	Planned/ reserved activity (N=235)	Completed activity (n=215)	Did not complete activity (n=20)	Activity completed as planned %
Cross country ski tour	15	11	4	73
Natural history tour (not ranger-guided)	9	9	0	100
Photography tour	12	8	4	67
Scenic motorized tour (other than snowcoach or snowmobile)	8	8	0	100
Snowcoach tour	99	94	5	95
Snowmobile tour	58	54	4	93
Snowshoe tour	2	2	0	100
Ski equipment rental	12	11	1	92
Snowshoe rental	11	10	1	91
Yellowstone Association Institute class	9	8	1	89

*total percentages do not equal 100 due to rounding

**total percentages do not equal 100 because visitors could select more than one answer

Importance ratings of concession services and activities used

Question 14c

For only those services and activities that your personal group used, please rate their importance to your visit from 1-5.

> 1=Not at all important
> 2=Slightly important
> 3=Moderately important
> 4=Very important
> 5=Extremely important

Results

- Table 27 shows the importance ratings of each concession service and activity. The concession services/activities that received the highest combined "extremely important" and "very important" ratings were:

  87% Snowcoach tour
  85% Snowmobile tour

- Results for concession services/activities rated by N<30 visitor groups may be unreliable.

Table 27. Importance ratings of concession services and activities used on this trip (N=number of visitor groups)

Concession service/activity	N	Rating (%)*				
		Not at all important	Slightly important	Moderately important	Very important	Extremely important
Cross country ski tour	12	0	0	25	25	50
Natural history tour (not ranger-guided)	14	0	0	14	50	36
Photography tour	9	0	0	0	33	67
Scenic motorized tour (other than snowcoach or snowmobile)	11	0	0	27	36	36
Snowcoach tour	122	0	1	12	39	48
Snowmobile tour	61	0	0	15	28	57
Snowshoe tour	16	0	0	13	63	25
Ski equipment rental	27	0	0	33	30	37
Snowshoe rental	14	0	0	21	50	29
Yellowstone Association Institute class	9	0	0	0	0	100

*total percentages do not equal 100 due to rounding
**total percentages do not equal 100 because visitors could select more than one answer

Quality ratings of concession services and activities used

Question 14d

For only those services and activities that your personal group used, please rate their quality from 1-5.

    1=Very poor
    2=Poor
    3=Average
    4=Good
    5=Very good

Results

- Table 28 shows the quality ratings of each concession service and activity. The concession services/activities rated by 30 or more visitor groups that received the highest combined "very good" and "good" ratings were:

    94% Snowmobile tour
    87% Snowcoach tour

- Results for concession services/activities rated by N<30 visitor groups may be unreliable.

Table 28. Quality ratings of concession services and activities
(N=number of visitor groups)

Concession service/activity	N	Rating (%)*				
		Very poor	Poor	Average	Good	Very good
Cross country ski tour	12	0	0	0	50	50
Natural history tour (not ranger-guided)	14	0	0	14	29	57
Photography tour	9	0	0	33	0	67
Scenic motorized tour (other than snowcoach or snowmobile)	11	0	0	27	36	36
Snowcoach tour	121	0	3	10	31	56
Snowmobile tour	61	2	0	5	28	66
Snowshoe tour	16	0	0	6	38	56
Ski equipment rental	27	0	0	15	56	30
Snowshoe rental	15	7	7	0	47	40
Yellowstone Association Institute class	9	0	0	0	0	100

*total percentages do not equal 100 due to rounding
**total percentages do not equal 100 because visitors could select more than one answer

Expenditures

Total expenditures inside and outside the park

Question 15

For your personal group, please report all expenditures for the items listed below for this visit to Yellowstone NP and the surrounding area (within 150 miles of the park).

Results

- 41% of visitor groups spent $1-$1000 (see Figure 58).

- 17% spent $1001-$2000.

- 14% spent $2001-$3000.

- The average visitor group expenditure was $2114.

- The median group expenditure (50% of groups spent more and 50% of groups spent less) was $1197.

- The average total expenditure per person (per capita) was $777.

- As shown in Figure 59, the largest proportions of total expenditures inside and outside the park were:

  30% Lodges, hotels, motels, cabins, B&Bs, etc.
  20% Snowmobiles and coaches
  18% Other transportation expenses

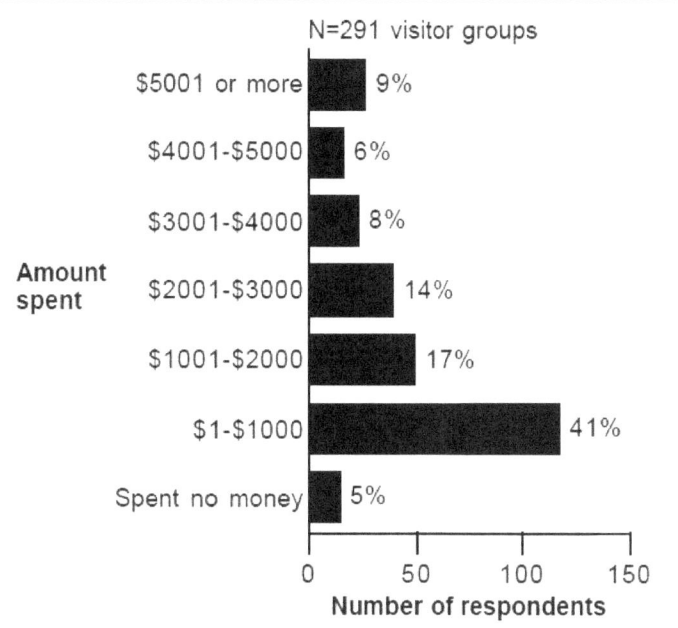

Figure 58. Total expenditures inside and outside the park

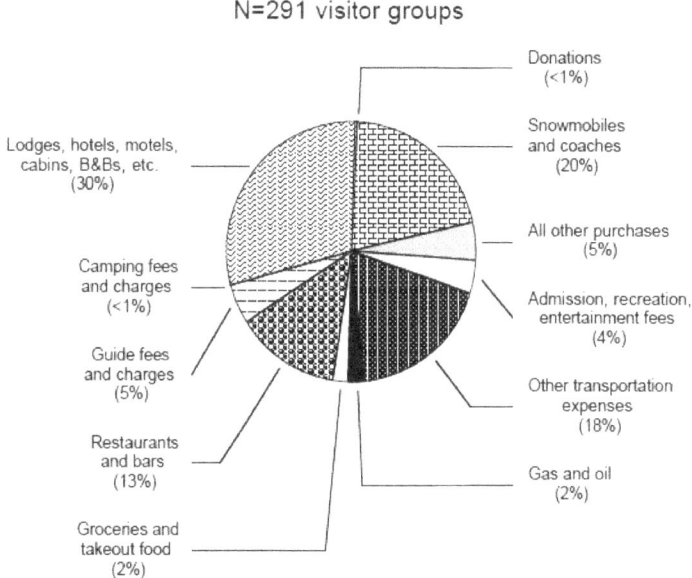

Figure 59. Proportions of total expenditures inside and outside the park

---

*total percentages do not equal 100 due to rounding

**total percentages do not equal 100 because visitors could select more than one answer

Number of adults covered by expenditures

Question 15c
How many adults (18 years or older) do
these expenses cover?

Results
- 60% of visitor groups had two adults
  covered by expenditures (see
  Figure 60).

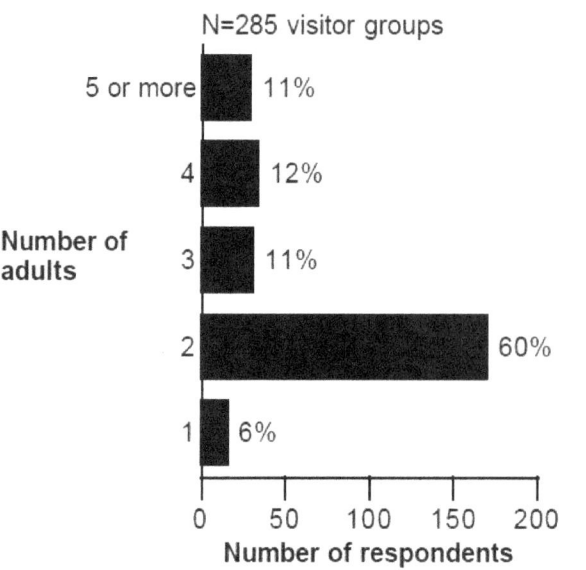

Figure 60. Number of adults covered by
expenditures

Number of children covered by expenditures

Question 15c
How many children (under 18 years) do
these expenses cover?

Results
- 82% of visitor groups had no children
  covered by expenditures (see
  Figure 61).

- 14% had one or two children.

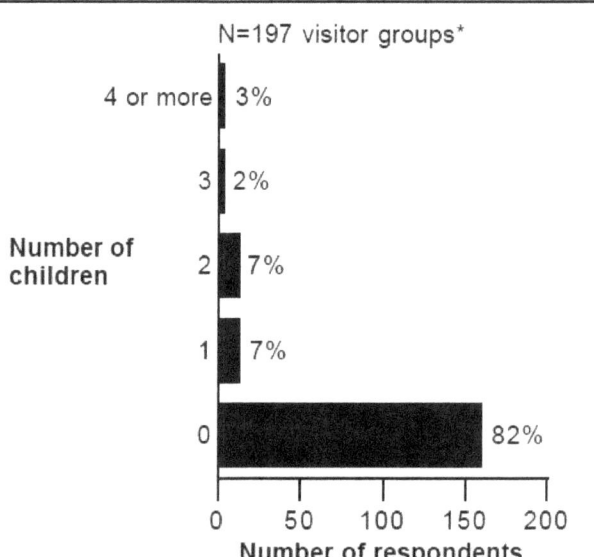

Figure 61. Number of children covered by
expenditures

---

*total percentages do not equal 100 due to rounding

**total percentages do not equal 100 because visitors could select more than one answer

Expenditures inside the park

Question 15a
Please list your personal group's total
expenditures inside Yellowstone NP.

Results

- 48% of visitor groups spent $1-$500
  (see Figure 62).

- 14% spent $501-$1000.

- 14% spent no money.

- The average visitor group expenditure
  inside the park was $750.

- The median group expenditure (50%
  of groups spent more and 50% of
  groups spent less) was $322.

- The average total expenditure per
  person (per capita) was $297.

- As shown in Figure 63, the largest
  proportions of total expenditures
  inside the park were:

    33% Lodges, hotels, motels,
        cabins, B&Bs, etc.
    26% Snowmobiles and coaches
    17% Restaurants and bars

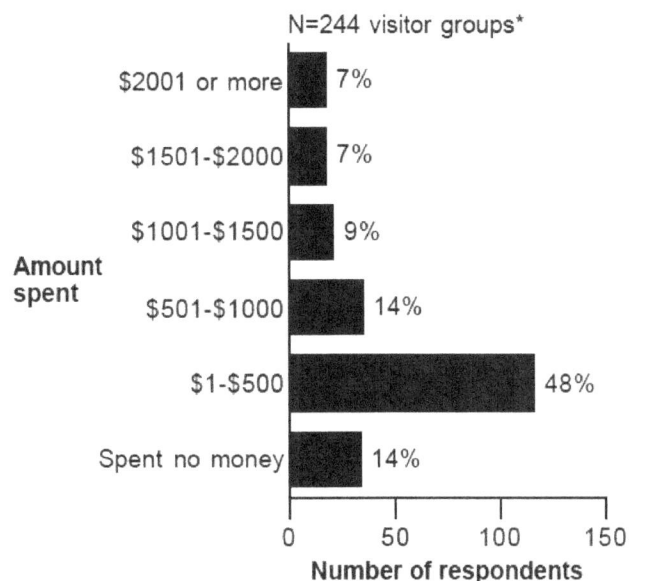

Figure 62. Total expenditures inside the park

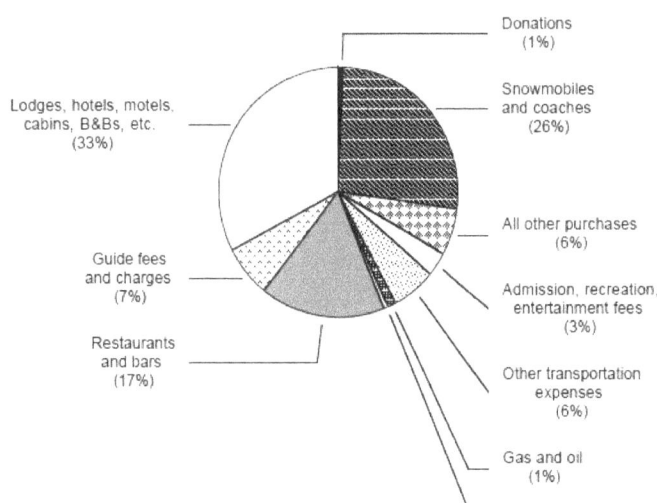

Figure 63. Proportions of total expenditures inside the
park

---

*total percentages do not equal 100 due to rounding

**total percentages do not equal 100 because visitors could select more than one answer

<u>Lodges, hotels, motels, cabins, B&Bs, etc.</u>

- 44% of visitor groups spent no money on lodges, hotels, motels, cabins, B&Bs, etc. inside the park (see Figure 64).

- 28% spent $1-$500.

- 18% spent $501-$1000.

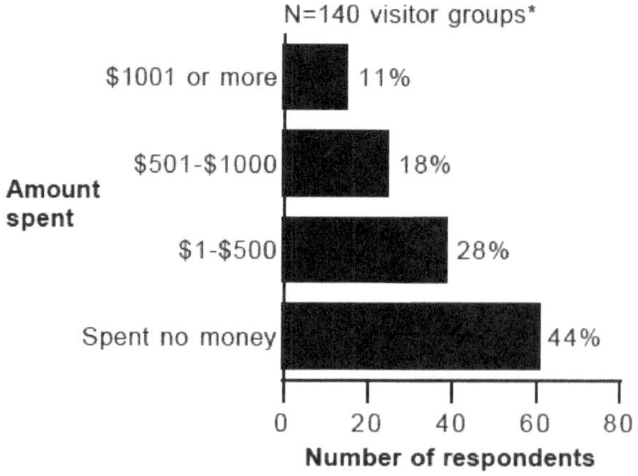

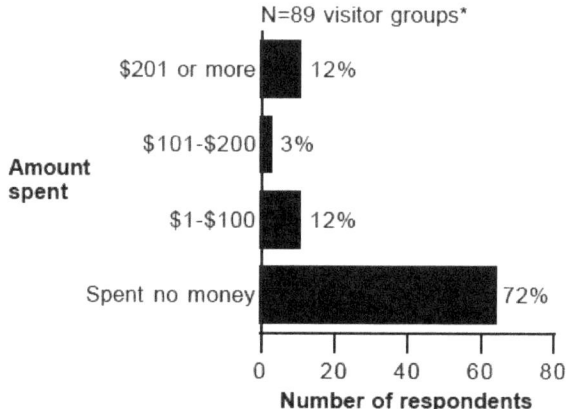

Figure 64. Expenditures for lodging inside the park

<u>Guide fees and charges</u>

- 72% of visitor groups spent no money on guide fees and charges inside the park (see Figure 65).

- 12% spent $1-$100.

- 12% spent $201 or more.

Figure 65. Expenditures for guide fees and charges inside the park

---

*total percentages do not equal 100 due to rounding

**total percentages do not equal 100 because visitors could select more than one answer

Restaurants and bars

- 26% of visitor groups spent $1-$50 on restaurants and bars inside the park (see Figure 66).

- 25% spent no money.

- 21% spent $201 or more.

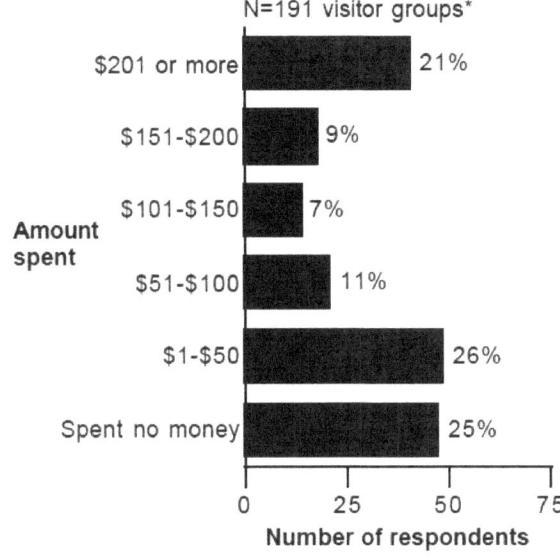

Figure 66. Expenditures for restaurants and bars inside the park

Groceries and takeout food

- 70% of visitor groups spent no money on groceries and takeout food inside the park (see Figure 67).

- 19% spent $1-$25.

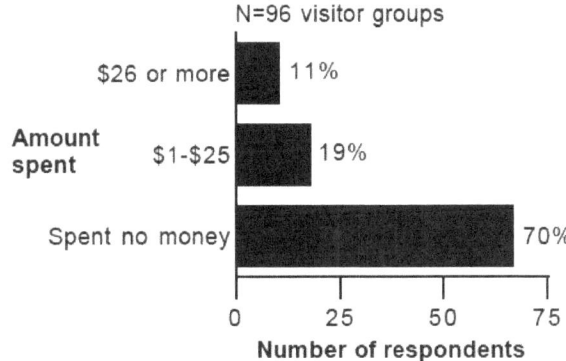

Figure 67. Expenditures for groceries and takeout food inside the park

---

*total percentages do not equal 100 due to rounding

**total percentages do not equal 100 because visitors could select more than one answer

Gas and oil (auto, RV, snowmobile, etc.)

- 84% of visitor groups spent no money on gas and oil inside the park (see Figure 68).

- 9% spent $51 or more.

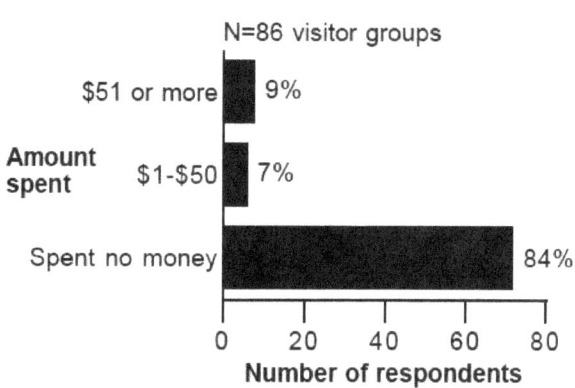

Figure 68. Expenditures for gas and oil inside the park

Other transportation expenses (including airfare, rental cars, auto repairs, etc.)

- 86% of visitor groups spent no money on other transportation expenses inside the park (see Figure 69).

- 8% spent $1-$500.

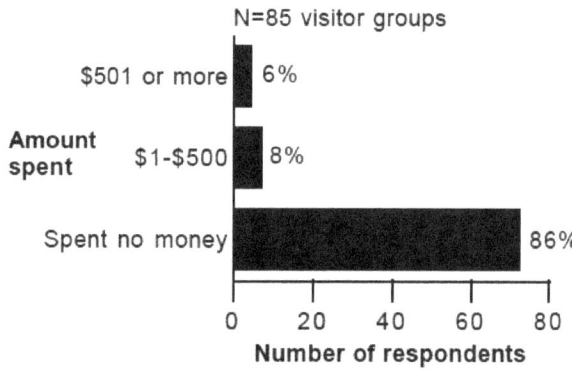

Figure 69. Expenditures for other transportation expenses inside the park

Admission, recreation, entertainment fees

- 51% of visitor groups spent no money on admission, recreation, or entertainment fees inside the park (see Figure 70).

- 19% spent $1-$25.

- 17% spent $51 or more.

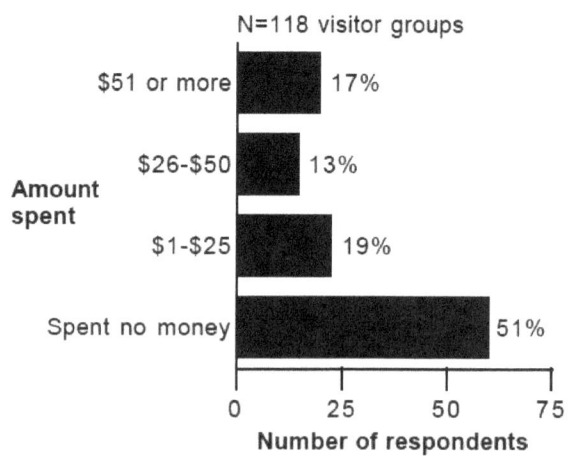

Figure 70. Expenditures for admission, recreation, or entertainment fees inside the park

---

*total percentages do not equal 100 due to rounding

**total percentages do not equal 100 because visitors could select more than one answer

All other purchases (souvenirs, film, books, sporting goods, clothing, etc.)

- 42% of visitor groups spent $1-$50 on all other purchases inside the park (see Figure 71).

- 30% spent no money.

- 15% spent $101 or more.

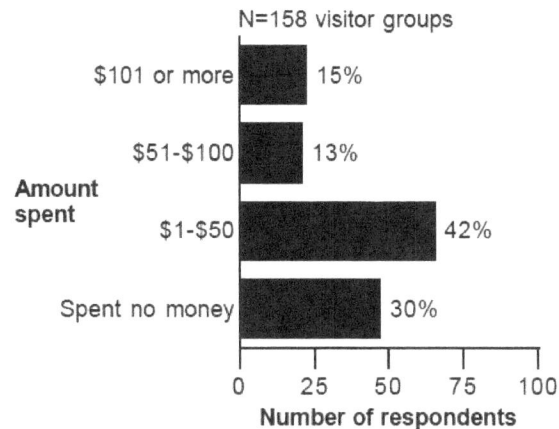

Figure 71. Expenditures for all other purchases inside the park

Snowmobiles and coaches

- 37% of visitor groups spent no money on snowmobiles and coaches inside the park (see Figure 72).

- 35% spent $301 or more.

- 13% spent $201-$300.

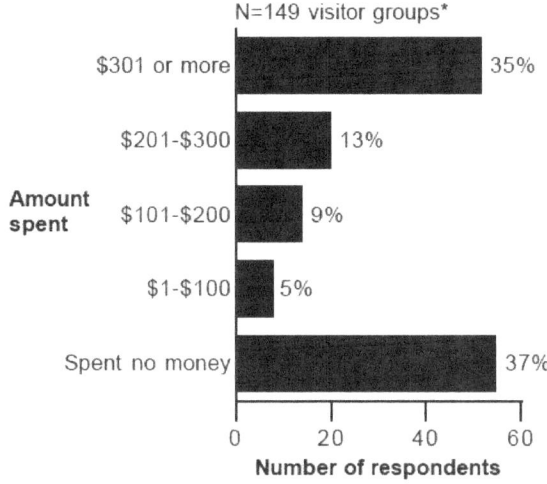

Figure 72. Expenditures for snowmobiles and coaches inside the park

Donations

- 66% of visitor groups spent no money on donations inside the park (see Figure 73).

- 24% spent $1-$25.

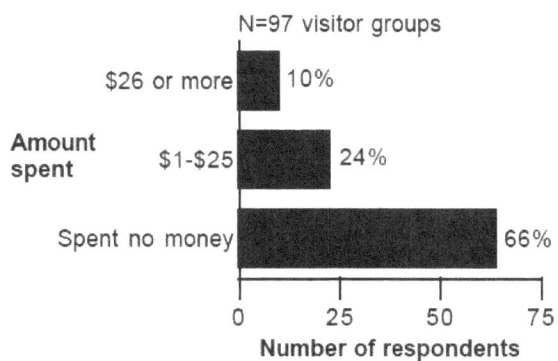

Figure 73. Expenditures for donations inside the park

*total percentages do not equal 100 due to rounding
**total percentages do not equal 100 because visitors could select more than one answer

Expenditures outside the park

Question 15b

Please list your personal group's total expenditures outside the park (within 150 miles).

Results

- 51% of visitor groups spent $1-$1000 (see Figure 74).

- 14% spent $1001-$2000.

- 12% spent $4001 or more.

- The average visitor group expenditure outside the park was $1808.

- The median group expenditure (50% of groups spent more and 50% of groups spent less) was $875.

- The average total expenditure per person (per capita) was $701.

- As shown in Figure 75, the largest proportions of total expenditures outside the park were:

    28% Lodges, hotels, motels, cabins, B&B, etc.
    23% Other transportation expenses
    18% Snowmobiles and coaches

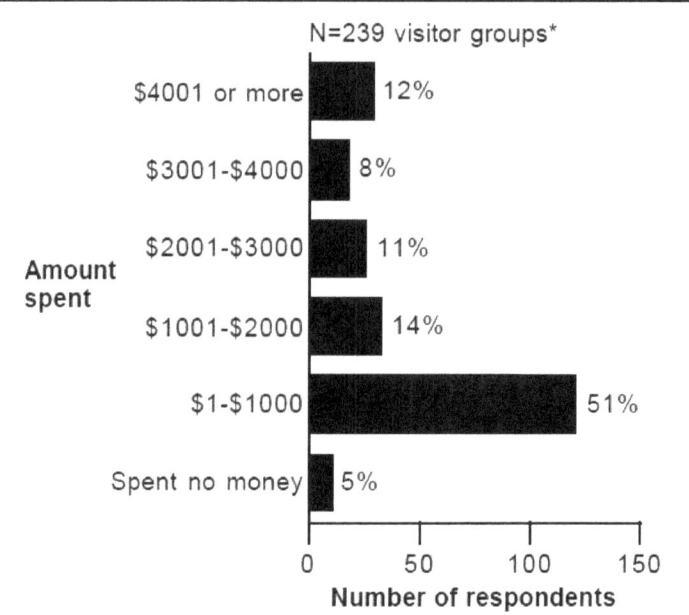

Figure 74. Total expenditures outside the park

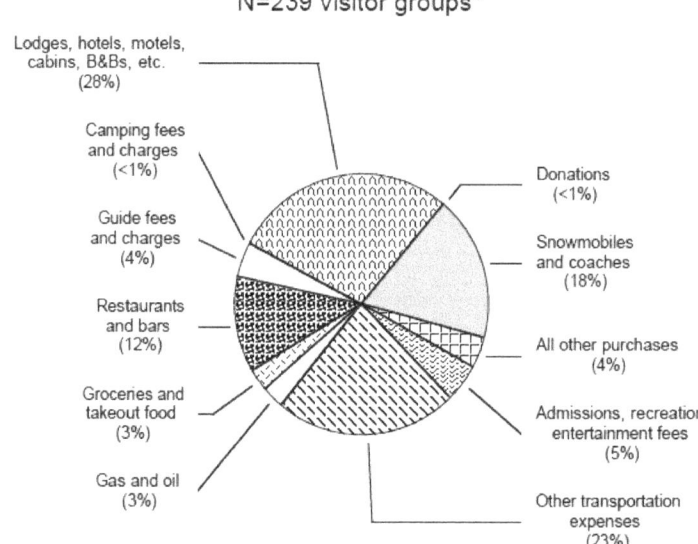

Figure 75. Proportions of total expenditures outside the park

---

*total percentages do not equal 100 due to rounding

**total percentages do not equal 100 because visitors could select more than one answer

<u>Lodges, hotels, motels, cabins, B&Bs, etc.</u>

- 56% of visitor groups spent $1-$500 on lodging outside the park (see Figure 76).

- 18% spent $501-$1000.

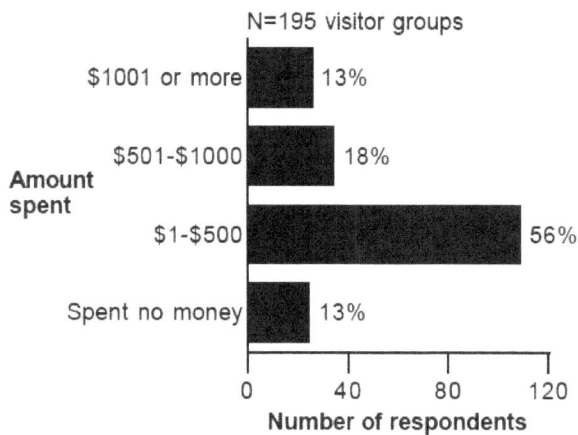

Figure 76. Expenditures for lodging outside the park

<u>Camping fees and charges</u>

- 97% of visitor groups spent no money on camping fees and charges outside the park (see Figure 77).

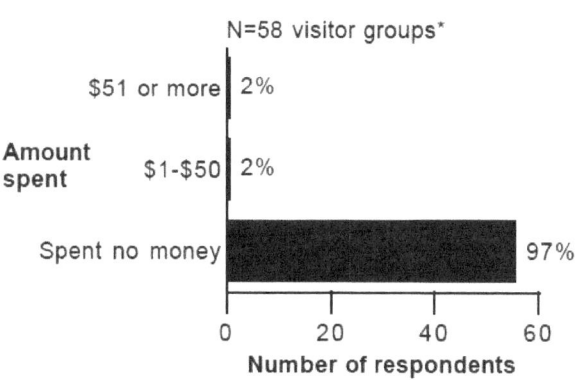

Figure 77. Expenditures for camping fees and charges outside the park

<u>Guide fees and charges</u>

- 60% of visitor groups spent no money on guide fees and charges outside the park (see Figure 78).

- 24% spent $201 or more.

- 11% spent $1-$100.

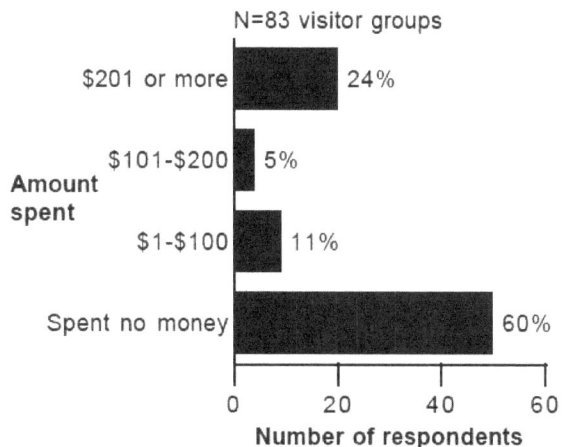

Figure 78. Expenditures for guide fees and charges outside the park

---

*total percentages do not equal 100 due to rounding

**total percentages do not equal 100 because visitors could select more than one answer

Restaurants and bars

- 37% of visitor groups spent $1-$100 on restaurants and bars outside the park (see Figure 79).

- 27% spent $301 or more.

- 22% spent $101-$200.

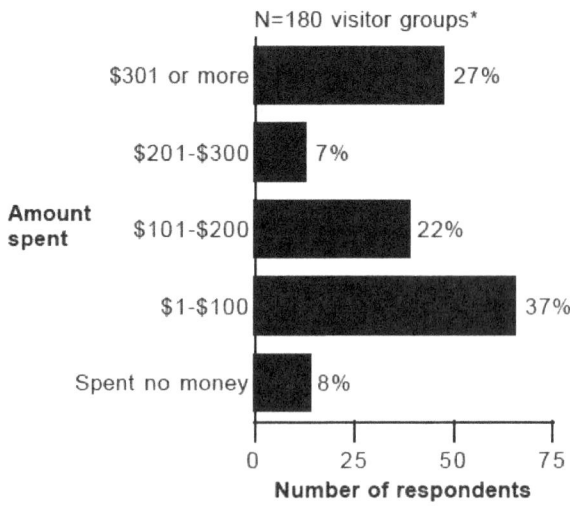

Figure 79. Expenditures for restaurants and bars outside the park

Groceries and takeout food

- 39% of visitor groups spent $1-$50 on groceries and takeout food outside the park (see Figure 80).

- 22% spent $51-$100.

- 20% spent no money.

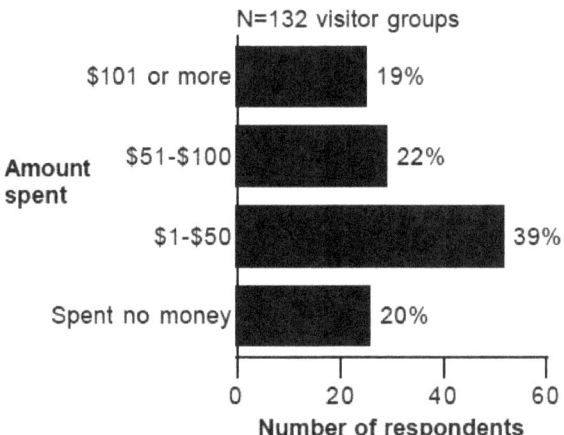

Figure 80. Expenditures for groceries and takeout food outside the park

---

*total percentages do not equal 100 due to rounding

**total percentages do not equal 100 because visitors could select more than one answer

Gas and oil (auto, RV, snowmobile, etc.)

- 34% of visitor groups spent $51-$100 on gas and oil outside the park (see Figure 81).

- 27% spent $1-$50.

- 20% spent no money.

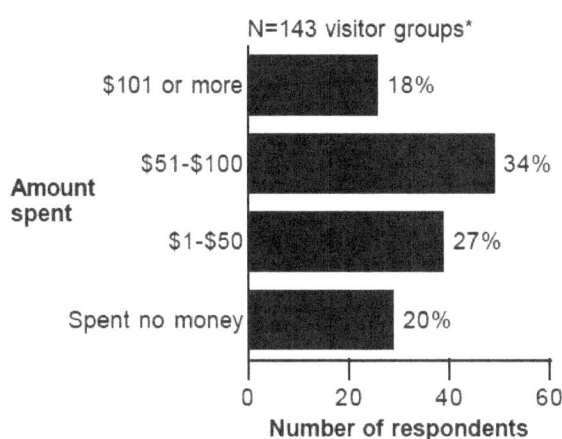

Figure 81. Expenditures for gas and oil outside the park

Other transportation (including airfare, rental cars, auto repairs, etc.)

- 34% of visitor groups spent no money on other transportation outside the park (see Figure 82).

- 23% spent $501-$1000.

- 20% spent $1-$500.

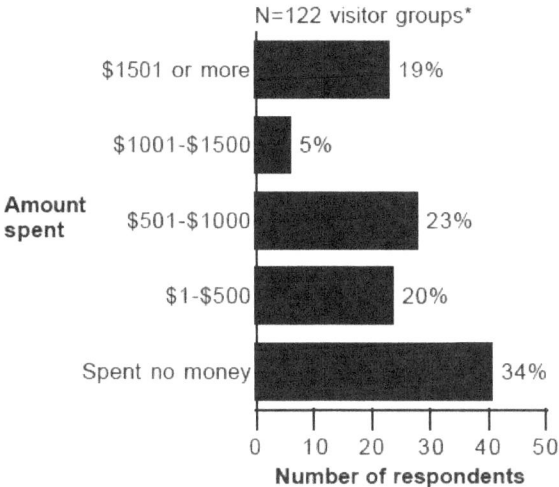

Figure 82. Expenditures for other transportation outside the park

*total percentages do not equal 100 due to rounding
**total percentages do not equal 100 because visitors could select more than one answer

69

Admission, recreation, entertainment fees

- 36% of visitor groups spent no money on admission, recreation, entertainment fees outside the park (see Figure 83).

- 28% spent $1-$50.

- 22% spent $101 or more.

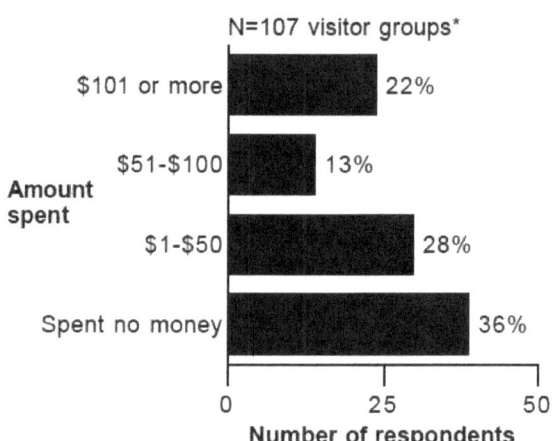

Figure 83. Expenditures for admission, recreation, entertainment fees outside the park

All other purchases (souvenirs, film, books, sporting goods, clothing, etc.)

- 30% of visitor groups spent $151 or more on all other purchases outside the park (see Figure 84).

- 29% spent $1-$50.

- 25% spent no money.

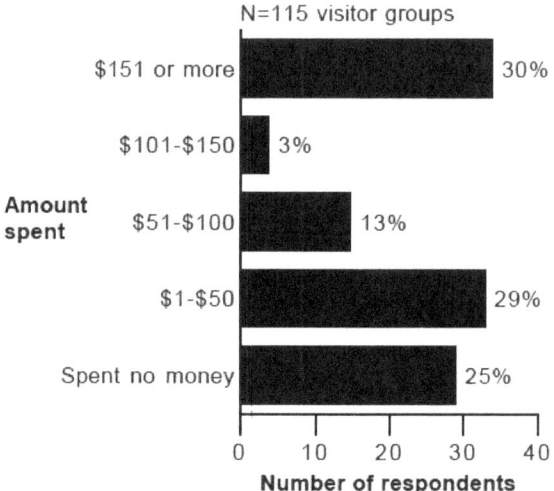

Figure 84. Expenditures for all other purchases outside the park

---

*total percentages do not equal 100 due to rounding

**total percentages do not equal 100 because visitors could select more than one answer

Snowmobiles and coaches

- 54% of visitor groups spent $301 or more on snowmobiles and coaches outside the park (see Figure 85).

- 24% spent no money.

- 15% spent $201-$300.

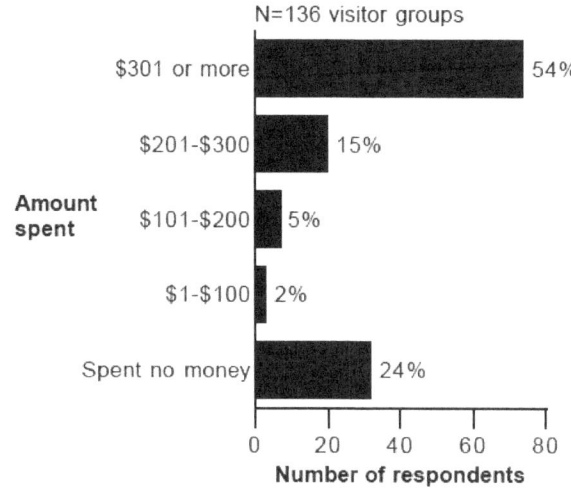

Figure 85. Expenditures for snowmobiles and coaches outside the park

Donations

- 79% of visitor groups spent no money on donations outside the park (see Figure 86).

- 11% spent $1-$25.

- 11% spent $26 or more.

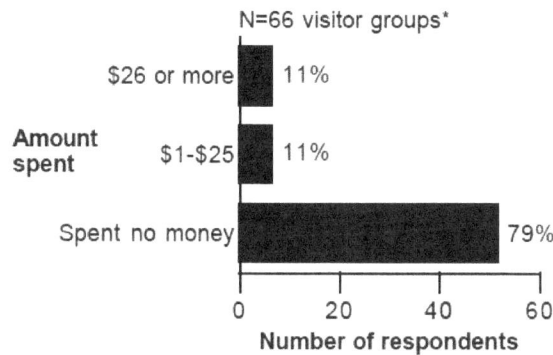

Figure 86. Expenditures for donations outside the park

*total percentages do not equal 100 due to rounding
**total percentages do not equal 100 because visitors could select more than one answer

Preferences for Future Visits

Cell phone service

Question 12a
On a future visit, would your personal group like to have cell phone services available in developed areas in Yellowstone NP?

Results
- 61% of visitor groups were interested in having cell phone service available in developed areas of the park (see Figure 87).

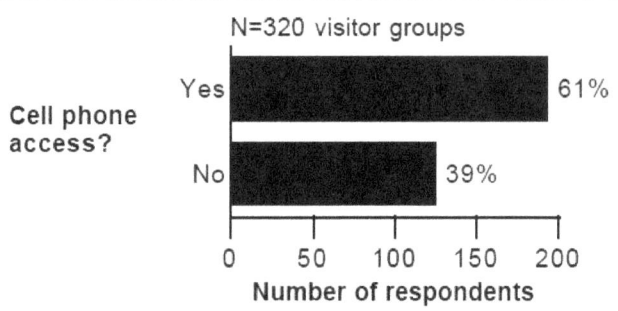

Figure 87. Visitor groups that desired cell phone services in developed areas of the park

Internet access

Question 12b
On a future visit, would your personal group like to have internet access available in developed areas in Yellowstone NP?

Results
- 49% of visitor groups desired internet access in developed areas of the park (see Figure 88).

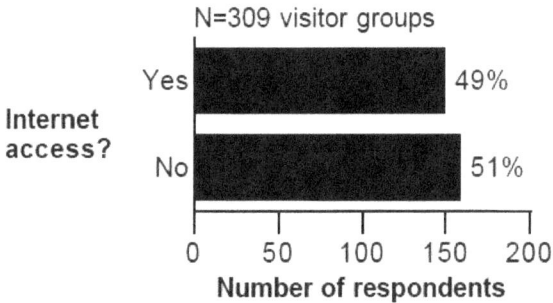

Figure 88. Visitor groups that desired internet access in developed areas of the park

Other services

Question 12c
On a future visit, would your personal group like to have other services available in developed areas in Yellowstone NP? (Open-ended)

Results – Interpret results with **CAUTION!**
- 4 visitor groups responded to this question.

- Table 29 shows "other" services desired in developed areas of the park.

Table 29. Other services visitor groups would like to have in developed areas of the park – **CAUTION!**

Services	Number of times mentioned
AT&T didn't work here	1
Free Wi-Fi	1
Guides	1
Television for children	1

---

*total percentages do not equal 100 due to rounding
**total percentages do not equal 100 because visitors could select more than one answer

Overall Quality

Question 26

Overall, how would you rate the quality of the facilities, services, and recreational opportunities provided to your personal group at Yellowstone NP during this visit?

Results

- 94% of visitor groups rated the overall quality of facilities, services, and recreational opportunities as "very good" or "good" (see Figure 89).

- 1% of visitor groups rated the quality as "very poor" or "poor."

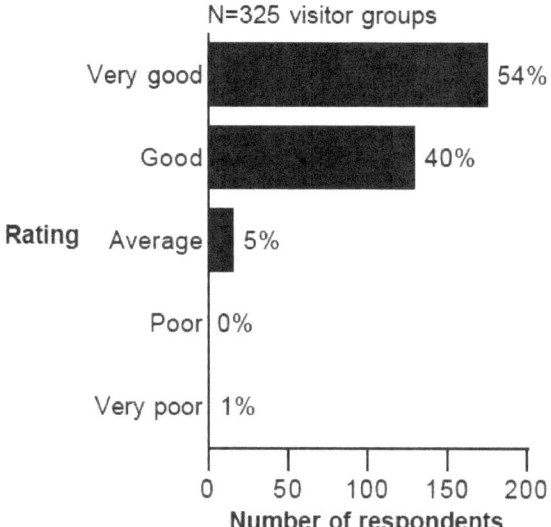

Figure 89. Overall quality rating of facilities, services, and recreational opportunities

---

*total percentages do not equal 100 due to rounding

**total percentages do not equal 100 because visitors could select more than one answer

Visitor Comment Summaries

What visitors liked most

Question 24a

Commercial services at Yellowstone NP include lodging, restaurants/food service, stores, gift shops, medical clinics, gas stations, snowcoach tours, snowmobile tours, etc. On this visit, what did your personal group like most about the commercial services? (Open-ended)

Results

- 80% of visitor groups (N=268) responded to this question.

- Table 30 shows a summary of visitor comments. The transcribed open-ended comments can be found in the Visitor Comments section.

Table 30. What visitors liked most
(N=386 comments; some visitor groups made more than one comment.)

Comment	Number of times mentioned
Personnel (22%)	
Friendly staff	34
Snowcoach tour guides	13
Tour guide	10
Knowledgeable staff	9
Helpful staff	7
Excellent snowmobile guides	4
Knowledgeable guides	4
Other comments	5
Interpretive Services (3%)	
Old Faithful Visitor Center exhibits	3
Ranger talk	3
Museum	2
Other comments	2
Facilities/Maintenance (4%)	
Clean	10
Visitor center	5
Other comments	2
Concession Services (55%)	
Snowcoach tour	60
Snowmobile tour	24
Lodging was good	22
Food was good	19
Restaurants	14
Tour	11
Snowmobiling	10
Gift shops	9
Old Faithful Snow Lodge	8
Ski shop/rental availability	6
Mammoth Hotel restaurant	4
Old Faithful restaurant	3

Table 30. What visitors liked most (continued)

Comment	Number of times mentioned
Concession Services (continued)	
Mammoth Hotel	2
Sitting around fireplace	2
Ski shuttle	2
Other comments	16
Policy/Management (1%)	
Great having winter access to park	2
Other comments	2
General (13%)	
Convenience of services	7
Did not use services	6
Accessibility of services	4
Reasonable prices	4
All excellent	3
All services were good	3
Well organized	3
I got the most for my money	2
Quality	2
Skiing	2
Other comments	14

What visitors liked least

Question 24b

On this visit, what did your personal group like least about the commercial services (lodging, restaurants/food service, stores, gift shops, medical clinics, gas stations, snowcoach tours, snowmobile tours, etc.)? (Open-ended)

Results

- 50% of visitor groups (N=156) responded to this question.

- Table 31 shows a summary of visitor comments. The transcribed open-ended comments can be found in the Visitor Comments section.

Table 31. What visitors liked least
(N=179 comments; some visitor groups made more than one comment.)

Comment	Number of times mentioned
Restaurants/Food Services (32%)	
Food	16
Restaurants	11
Limited selection of food in restaurants	8
Prices too high	6
Limited choices of restaurants	3
Long waiting time at restaurants	3
Food prices and service	2
Need more restaurants	2
Not enough seating in restaurant	2
Other comments	4
Lodging (16%)	
Room too warm	5
Mammoth Lodge needs updating	4
Mammoth Lodge temperature too variable	3
Prices too high	3
Hard to get reservations	2
Lodging	2
Other comments	9
Guided Tours (19%)	
Snowcoach broke down/disrepair	5
Too many snowmobiles in park	5
Snowmobiles having to be guided	4
Noisy snowmobiles/snowcoaches	2
Should be able to visit park with private vehicle	2
Snowcoach not up to expectations	2
Snowcoach crowded/group too big	2
Snowmobile tours	2
Tour was longer than expected	2
Other comments	8

Table 31. What visitors liked least (continued)

Comment	Number of times mentioned
Facilities/Maintenance (8%)	
Lack of cell phone service	3
Lack of internet service	3
Signage and directions not sufficient	3
Unplowed/ungroomed boardwalks & sidewalks	2
Other comments	4
General (25%)	
Nothing - all great/adequate	14
Closed services in winter	7
Prices too high	5
Bad customer service	3
Other comments	16

Additional comments

Question 25

Is there anything else your personal group would like to tell us about your visit to Yellowstone NP? (Open-ended)

Results

- 59% of visitor groups (N=186) responded to this question.

- Table 32 shows a summary of visitor comments. The transcribed open-ended comments can be found in the Visitor Comments section.

Table 32. Additional comments
(N=289 comments; some visitor groups made more than one comment.)

Comment	Number of times mentioned
Personnel (10%)	
Friendly staff	8
Tour guide was great	6
Excellent staff	4
Helpful staff	3
Staff was not attentive	2
Other comments	5
Interpretive services (4%)	
More programs or organized activities	4
Enjoyed the ranger talks	3
Other comments	4
Facilities/Maintenance (9%)	
More developed restrooms	5
Bathrooms were convenient and clean	3
Nicely groomed ski trails	3
Signs on ski trails not sufficient	3
Visitor center was great	3
Want more cellular coverage in the park	2
Wished more facilities were open	2
Other comments	5
Concession Services (18%)	
Snowcoach tour was great	4
Guided tour not up to expectations	2
Liked music at Mammoth	2
Liked ski drop service	2
Mammoth Hot Springs Hotel was too hot	2
Old Faithful Snow Lodge was excellent	3
Snowcoach was too expensive	2
Snowmobiles were great	2
Snowshoe tour was the best	2
We had a great tour	3
Yellowstone Association runs a great program	2
Other comments	25

Table 32. Additional comments (continued)

Comment	Number of times mentioned
Policy/Management (18%)	
Allow snowmobiles without tour guides	9
Continue to allow snowmobiles in the park	7
Access to the park in winter is critical	6
Continue to control snowmobile tours	6
Limit the number of people in park in winter	4
Allow more car traffic throughout park	2
Limit commercial services/no more new services	2
More trails for snowmobiles/off road access	2
Other comments	14
Resource Management (3%)	
Continue to protect the resources	3
Protect the resource for the animals not for people	2
Wolf population is too big, harming the elk/other wildlife	2
Other comments	2
General (16%)	
Loved our experience in the park	29
Had a great time	15
We will come back	9
Great winter experience	8
NPS does a great job, thanks, keep it up	7
Seeing all the wildlife was wonderful	7
Great comparison to summer visit	6
Beautiful park	5
Exceeded our expectations	4
Park is beautiful in winter	4
Always enjoy it	3
Memorable experience of a lifetime	3
Enjoyed the quiet atmosphere	2
Enjoyed the thermal features/geysers	2
Loved the skiing	2
Other comments	7

Visitor Comments

This section contains visitor responses to open-ended questions.

Question 24a
   On this visit, what did you and your personal group like most about the commercial services?
   (Open-ended)

- A lot of information, nice people, heated seats, handles
- Access to the lodge for food and museum
- Adequate for the time of the year; all excellent
- All of the above (minus medical clinics which didn't use)
- All of the above through National Geographic
- All services were good with the exceptions of the snowcoach and lodging - there were a few mix-ups
- All the employees were incredibly nice and helpful
- Although we didn't use it, I appreciated knowing there was medical if needed
- Atmosphere and preserving integrity of old buildings
- Availability
- Availability and ease of use
- Baggage handling was excellent, meals provided were appreciated
- Beautiful scenery
- Clean
- Clean
- Clean
- Clean and nice; snowmobiling and snowcoach people were very nice
- Clean facilities and very accommodating employees
- Clean, quiet, convenient
- Coffee shop in Mammoth hotel
- Comfort of snowcoach and personnel
- Convenience
- Convenience
- Convenience and products connected to place
- Convenience in the location and accessibility of existing services; we also appreciate that the existing services are restricted to a few places inside YNP
- Convenient
- Did not use them
- Did not use, only used restrooms
- Didn't go to any
- Didn't really need it
- Didn't use any other than snow coach tour
- Didn't use because it was winter
- Everyone very helpful
- Everyone was very nice and helpful
- Everything connected with the snowcoach
- Everything was fine
- Excellent

- Excellent choice and variety of books and videos; Driver/guide on snowcoach tour
- Excellent restaurant
- Excellent accommodations at the Snow Lodge at Old Faithful; the ski shuttle from Old Faithful
- Food service
- Food variety, gift shop selection, knowledgeable, engaging guides
- Food was great. Nice to be able to have cocktails.
- Friendliness of Xanterra snowcoach drivers
- Friendliness, ease of use
- Friendly and felt I got the most for my money
- Friendly and knowledgeable staffing
- Friendly and very knowledgeable people
- Friendly service
- Friendly service
- Friendly service
- Friendly staff by Xanterra
- Friendly staff, lobby of Snow Lodge for relaxing, visiting
- Friendly, helpful staff
- Friendly, informative guide
- Gift shop
- Gift shop
- Gift shops
- Gift shops
- Gift shops, restaurant
- Gifts shops, ranger talk, museum, snowcoach tours
- Good food
- Good food and friendly staff
- Good food at Mammoth Hotel dining area
- Good food, great coach tour
- Good food; friendly wait staff, clerks and YNP employees
- Good guides, many stops to take pictures, got to see a lot of the park
- Good value
- Great new visitor center, bookstore, YA staff
- Great snowcoach tour guide "Swany"
- Guided tour/snowcoach and tour guide
- Guides were all so knowledgeable and took time to answer all our questions
- Having a very knowledgeable guide
- High quality, well-maintained, well staffed
- Hot tub
- Icy boardwalks
- Incredibly friendly and knowledgeable people
- Indifferent
- Informative tour
- It was open - we went thinking everything was closed for the winter
- Knowledge of guide

- Knowledge of the coach drivers
- Knowledgeable and friendly
- Knowledgeable and friendly staff
- Knowledgeable, friendly staff, well-trained. Facilities clean and well kept.
- Knowledgeable, friendly, attune to adventurous guests
- Lecture from ranger at Old Faithful
- Lodge, Snow, Old Faithful
- Lodge, snowcoach bombardier, skiing
- Lodges were great, food was very good and snowmobile tour was excellent
- Lodges were nice and well run
- Lodges were nice, food good, cozy fireplaces
- Lodging
- Lodging
- Lodging
- Lodging and food were great - staff very friendly
- Lodging and snowmobile
- Lodging good, visitor centers great, food and bars good
- Lodging was an expected
- Lodging, ski services, rental and drops
- Lodging, Visitors Center
- Lodging/food
- Loved the detail and attention of snow coach tour
- Mammoth Hotel Restaurant and food service
- Mammoth Hotel, snowmobile tour was great. Restaurant. How few people there were was good. Warming huts were nice for those that got cold.
- Mammoth Restaurant and snowcoach
- Narration on snowcoach tour - knowledgeable guide
- New items on breakfast menu at Old Faithful
- Old Faithful exhibition
- Old Faithful Snow Lodge
- Old Faithful Snow Lodge cabins
- Old Faithful visitor center
- Old Faithful Visitor Center is attractive, informative and clean
- Only did snowmobile tour
- Our tour guide, Dave
- Our tour guide, Suzi does her job well
- Park ranger
- Personal, friendly representatives working
- Price and location of Mammoth Hotel
- Quality, selection, concern
- Reasonable cost
- Reasonable prices
- Restaurant
- Restaurant and bar
- Restaurant and lodge

- Restaurant at Mammoth
- Restaurant food
- Restaurants able to accommodate for gluten free diet
- Restaurants, snowcoach, guides
- Restaurants/food
- Restaurants/food
- Service
- Simplicity
- Sitting around fireplace, ice skating
- Ski rental
- Ski shop
- Skiing and snowcoach tour
- Skiing with guide
- Snowcoach guide was friendly and informative
- Snow Lodge and rooms beautiful - great dining room food although pricey
- Snow Lodge had great places to relax; snowcoach tours - wonderful scenery, great guides
- Snow Lodge was a great getaway from work/TV
- Snowcoach
- Snowcoach
- Snowcoach
- Snowcoach
- Snowcoach
- Snowcoach
- Snowcoach - very friendly, informative, clean and relaxing
- Snowcoach service into park because it made it accessible with kids
- Snowcoach tour
- Snowcoach tour
- Snowcoach tour
- Snowcoach tour
- Snowcoach tour
- Snowcoach tour
- Snowcoach tour
- Snowcoach tour
- Snowcoach tour
- Snowcoach tour
- Snowcoach tour
- Snowcoach tour
- Snowcoach tour
- Snowcoach tour
- Snowcoach tour
- Snowcoach tour
- Snowcoach tour
- Snowcoach tour
- Snowcoach tour

- Snowcoach tour
- Snowcoach tour
- Snowcoach tour
- Snowcoach tour
- Snowcoach tour - Alpen Guides
- Snowcoach tour - best way to see Yellowstone in winter
- Snowcoach tour and snowmobile tour
- Snowcoach tour was fantastic
- Snowcoach tour, ski rentals availability
- Snowcoach tour; food and medicine were nice to be there, but not "most like"
- Snowcoach tours
- Snowcoach tours
- Snowcoach tours
- Snowcoach tours
- Snowcoach tours
- Snowcoach tours
- Snowcoach tours and guides
- Snowcoach tours, stores
- Snowcoach tours/ski shop
- Snowcoach, visitor center
- Snowmobile
- Snowmobile
- Snowmobile
- Snowmobile
- Snowmobile - excellent guide
- Snowmobile best through snowcoach
- Snowmobile tour
- Snowmobile tour
- Snowmobile tour
- Snowmobile tour
- Snowmobile tour
- Snowmobile tour
- Snowmobile tour
- Snowmobile tour
- Snowmobile tour
- Snowmobile tour
- Snowmobile tour
- Snowmobile tour was fantastic
- Snowmobile tour, food
- Snowmobile tour, restaurants
- Snowmobile tours
- Snowmobile tours
- Snowmobile tours
- Snowmobile tours were great; guide for snowmobile tours very knowledgeable

- Snowmobile/snowcoach tours
- Snowmobiles
- Snowmobiling
- Snowmobiling
- Snowmobiling - fresh air, great guide named Mike
- Stores/gift shops
- The Canyon tour with Zac
- The efforts of coordination with the park service
- The food and lodge were wonderful
- The guide on the snowcoach
- The guide was wonderful
- The housing inside West Yellowstone
- The International Buffet
- The Lodge
- The lodging and food were good
- The Mammoth Hotel and restaurant are exceptional and the concessions are very conservation oriented
- The new museum
- The snow coach tours
- The snowcoach tour - it was phenomenal. Very educational, got to see the park in a whole different state. We loved it!
- The snowcoach tour was very good at seeing we were taken care of
- The staff - everybody wanted to to be there and were very hospitable
- The staff almost always very friendly and outgoing
- The tour guides, who were really good
- Tour
- Tour guide Richard
- Tour, food, lodging, souvenirs
- Tours and wildlife watching
- Very efficient, organized, clean
- Very friendly
- Very friendly service
- Very friendly service
- Very good
- Very helpful and clean
- Viewing wildlife park in winter
- Visitor center
- Wait staff was terrific, buffet breakfast very fast, very nice and reasonably priced gift shop
- Warm inviting staff all very knowledgeable and helpful
- Warmth
- We like to stay in the lodge, love the historical perspective. Also enjoy eating in the dining room.
- We liked all of them but the best was the Steam and Stars tour
- We liked that everything was taken care of for our snowmobile trip
- We loved the guide and the Bombardier

- We loved the snowshoe tour/rental; it was highlight. Ranger talks: daytime and evening. Ice skating, but keep ice snow clear.
- Well organized
- Well organized, friendly, informative
- Wildlife
- Wildlife and attraction viewing via snowmobile
- Winter access to the park via snowmobiling for sightseeing and wildlife viewing
- Wolf Discovery Tour
- Wonderful happy/friendly service
- X-country ski rental and lodging
- Xanterra has great staff; snowcoach drivers are careful, hotel staff is efficient
- Yellowstone Adventures was fabulous; Kent and Van are great; very pleased with the new, more fuel efficient snowmobiles; the chili at Old Faithful restaurant
- Yellowstone Association Tour

Question 24b
On this visit, what did you and your personal group like least about the commercial services (lodging, restaurants/food service, stores, gift shops, medical clinics, gas stations, etc.) in Yellowstone NP? (Open-ended)

- A bit too expensive; if it was cheaper I would do it again
- All good
- All services adequate
- All that we had was acceptable; no need to add more
- Badly trained staff at the hotel, rental, store
- Cell phone, internet availability
- Closed in winter
- Cold/hot temperature differences at Mammoth Lodge - dining in separate building and had to go out in the weather
- Cost and limited availability of these tours to enter the park
- Cost, but that is to be expected
- Could provide more food, seating area indoors in Madison
- Dasani water has many salts for people with kidney problems
- Did not use
- Dinner selection in Obsidian dining room could be more family oriented
- Do not like Xanterra - it destroys the personal atmosphere of the stay - everything is homogenized
- Don't like the number of snowmobiles (too many), nor the way the bison had to hurry and move because of road traffic
- Expensive food
- Food
- Food
- Food
- Food
- Food at Old Faithful
- Food at Snow Lodge was expensive for quality. Dislike crowds of snowmobile along road to West Yellowstone
- Food at Snowlodge dining room way overpriced; lack of reasonably priced entrees on dinner menu
- Food in hotel
- Food just ok
- Food service
- Food service - multiple problems
- Food service was limited at Old Faithful, so there was a long line and wait time. That being said, it took away from our time on the boardwalk.
- Food was disappointing - doesn't need to be fancier, but it should be good quality, not bulk purchased such as bread, jelly, etc. Since there aren't any options, the food should be tasty
- Gas - stops after $30
- Gas prices
- Gas station
- Great trip; liked or enjoyed everything
- Group was too big
- Hard to find ski shop - signage and directions could be improved - helpful folks there

o   Hard to get snowmobile reservation
o   High prices
o   I thought everything was top notch
o   Internet/cell phone service at hotels
o   Just as hard to pick most as least. Everything met or exceeded expectations.
o   Just the snowcoach could have been a little better
o   Knowledgeable and friendly
o   Leaving
o   Limit food choices; tour was canceled but we were not informed until we were supposed to leave
o   Limited menu
o   Limited restaurant choices due to season
o   Lobby area in Mammoth not as good for visiting with people
o   Lodging
o   Lodging - bed is too small
o   Lodging and food expensive; don't increase snowmobile numbers - too many as is
o   Lodging at Mammoth Hotel: room was stuffy, hard to control heating, plugs were loose, shower temperature hard to control
o   Loved the snowcoach and the guides but very crowded seating, day long Canyon tour had 2-hr breakdown
o   Mammoth Hot Springs map room needs to have better environment for groups to sit, read, relax
o   Mammoth Hotel is not nearly as nice as Glacier Park services
o   Mammoth Hotel not inhabitable in winter
o   Mammoth Lodge rooms could be updated
o   Mammoth Springs Hotel was too hot (in February) and had plumbing problems
o   Many services/stores were closed
o   Money spent for snowcoach
o   More driving access in winter (i.e. snowcoach monopoly!)
o   Music in Mammoth Restaurant
o   Need to make early restaurant reservations, but I understand why, especially in winter
o   No bathtub in room. Room was quite warm.
o   No cell or internet service; heat in room
o   No dislikes at all
o   No individual snowmobiles in park
o   No overviews of tours or organized activities available
o   No pet boarding anywhere
o   No sunshine
o   No vegetarian restaurants/more restaurants
o   None
o   None - We loved YNP
o   Not being able to ride own snowmobile into the park without a guide
o   Not enough knowledge given from guide on NP/wildlife, etc.
o   Not enough open
o   Not enough restaurants/stores/food services open
o   Not enough seats at restaurant
o   Not much open during our time there

- Not signing up for collision insurance on snowmobile - painful lesson
- Nothing
- Nothing
- Nothing
- Nothing
- Old Faithful fast food restaurant did not have enough seating
- One complaint about lodging. Others in group had adequate rooms and we all paid the same
- One of the snowcoach drivers who talked every minute of the ride from Mammoth to Old Faithful
- One tour took an hour longer than had been listed, and having Parkinson's and trying to regulate medications hard
- Only spent 15-20 min at Canyon Village
- Our group is unhappy that we were stopped to be asked to complete the survey immediately on arrival
- Over-cooked meals
- Portions too big at restaurants; lights could be brighter for reading in rooms
- Prices
- Prices were a little high
- Prices, limited menu in Obsidian dining room
- Quality of heating at Lodges
- Restaurant
- Restaurant
- Restaurant
- Restaurant
- Restaurant at Mammoth Hot Springs
- Restaurant business (esp at breakfast)
- Restaurant food
- Restaurant food - not much
- Restaurant lines very long in winter
- Restaurant too crowded
- Restaurant/food service
- Restaurants
- Restaurants
- Restaurants
- Restaurants - horrible service
- Restaurants and hotels are fancy and expensive
- Restaurants good, but limited selections
- Restaurants/food service - nothing healthy
- Restaurants/food service need more open
- Restaurants/too many individual (personal) snowmobiles inside park
- Restrooms not enough
- Roads were not well-maintained
- Service at restaurant in park was slow
- Shower heads at Mammoth need some TLC
- Signage on ski trails, absence of walking only trails around Old Faithful Snow Lodge/cabins, etc.
- Snowcoach broke down and almost missed Old Faithful

o   Snowcoach on ride out (bus style) was quite noisy
o   Snowcoach tour
o   Snowcoach tours
o   Snowcoach was falling apart and side door even opened while we were moving
o   Snowmobile noise
o   Snowmobile tour
o   Snowmobile tours
o   Snowmobile was fun but too long
o   Snowmobiles having to be guided
o   Snowmobiles needed tour guides - if not we would have snowmobiled in the park and gone to more areas
o   Some attractions closed for winter season
o   The fact that they told us the snowcoach broke down and they had just fixed it
o   The food quality was quite average
o   The food selection was minimal at Old Faithful
o   The food was pretty bad
o   The gift shop wasn't open on Canyon tour
o   The new steel framed building facing Old Faithful is extremely poor design - does not fit into existing theme
o   The only problem we had was contacting the front desk from the cabin phone late
o   The restaurant - no options for dinner meals for cost and timing
o   The service of a particular waitress at the Obsidian dining room
o   The snowcoach ride was very long and it was over 50% of our time at park
o   Toilet size at Mammoth; icy paths between Lodge and Old Faithful
o   Too many snowcoaches
o   Too many snowmobiles; allow only 2/day
o   Too much heat in rooms at Mammoth
o   Unable to get the services we wanted
o   Unclear, infrequent signage to XC trailhead
o   Very hot room in Mammoth Hotel
o   Waiting in line for restrooms
o   Walking through unplowed/un-groomed boardwalks and sidewalks
o   Walkways in geyser areas packed with snow did not always seem safe
o   We didn't like it at all - too commercialized. Paying well over $100 to go to Old Faithful, I should be able to go there in my own vehicle
o   We made dinner reservations 3 months in advance and couldn't get in before 8:45. After our initial package we changed to the Frosty Fun package. I can't tell what the final charge was or any refunds as the billing was confusing.
o   We visited the park on a Saturday and Sunday. Both days we arrived for breakfast. Day 2, Sunday, we were disappointed that the menu options were different from Saturday. Since we were not interested in the Sunday buffet, options were too limited
o   West Yellowstone accommodation prices - ended up staying in my car

Question 25
Is there anything else you and your personal group would like to tell us about your visit to Yellowstone NP? (Open-ended)

o   Ability to move around inside park without guides... either drive in, snowmobile, etc., or ride in a via van/bus to Old Faithful at reasonable price

o   Always enjoy it, will keep coming back

o   Appreciated the availability of restrooms

o   Bathroom facilities were convenient and clean – thanks. Service for lunch was slow at the Snow Lodge

o   Be able to ride a snowmobile by ourselves

o   Beautiful and exciting six days. Park is so "fire and ice." Excellent change of pace from summer visits. All staff very attentive.

o   Beautiful National Park

o   Better services; would have liked more stores and restaurants open; local mechanics not helpful when we needed assistance with our snowmobile

o   Business outside of park had numerous complaints about Park Service stopping personal snowmobiles from entering the park; claim it is destroying business - a lot of businesses closed

o   Cannot imagine who would authorize the architecture use for both new buildings at Old Faithful - who got paid off to do the contract

o   Congratulations for the entire staff, rangers, snowcoach drivers, hotel and restaurant staff, all commercial staff; it is clear that the NP Superintendent keeps all commercial services under control

o   Continue to allow limited snowmobile tours as at present

o   Continue to keep the park open in the winter - it's beautiful and continue to allow snowmobiles in the park

o   Cull the bison herd; protect the natural balance and protection and reduce the business interest of increasing the number of tourists

o   Entry fees were appropriate; we are grateful tax dollars support national parks - we enjoyed the recreation - more amenities

o   Everyone was nice

o   Everything about visit was fine - I can find no fault with the way things were run

o   Exceeded expectations compare to various other vacations

o   Excellent staff, we really enjoyed our visit

o   Expectation for Old Faithful to burst up 200 feet in the air, however, it only went about 20' - explain that to your kids

o   Extend the snowcoach season to start earlier on Dec 1, if possible

o   Fantastic

o   Fantastic

o   Fantastic meals at Mammoth Dining Room - our compliments to the chef

o   Fantastic!

o   First winter visit; it was beautiful

o   Fix the heat in Mammoth Hotel

o   Food prices and service

o   Got best wolf info from a person at Super 8 - guest volunteer. Wolf sightings fun; show a little (??). Crowds not bad, Boiling River was fun; mostly young people; friendly folks on scopes watching wolves; so much better than a summer trip

o   Great

- Great staff: John, Kentucky; Eugene, Tennessee (drivers); Lindsay, Iowa (snowmobile guide), Shannon, Tennessee (snowmobile shop)
- Great trip
- Great trip. The National Park Service does a great job. Excellent job on the visitor centers.
- Guide complained too much about the wolves (we love wolves)
- Had a really nice time, thanks
- Hotel is great, but our room 128 shower would not hold constant water temperature; changed from very hot to very cold every 10 seconds
- I am very impressed with the strong conservation messages everywhere in the facilities from the recycling, the energy efficiency and the repeated messages about climate change and how it can change the park drastically for the worse.
- I participated in a National Geographic tour and feel many questions could not be answered very well; observation indicated a great park with good to excellent facilities
- I was concerned about local economics; that I would not have access to the park because of restrictions; many people are probably not coming because they believe they will not be able to enter the park
- I was surprised at how quiet the snowmobiles were; we did not ride them, but I think they should continue to be allowed
- I'd like to see more "off road" areas of the park - using service roads, etc., in the winter, either by snowcoach or snowmobile
- I've been to the Park 16 years in a row; we had a lot of fun in the early years with no guide; not so much fun with a guide - you do not have to be guided in the summer, why in the winter
- Impressed with staff friendliness; dining room, lodge, bookstore, visitor center
- Improve food quality, especially at Mammoth; some very unfriendly front desk staff at Mammoth
- In 2000 we worked at Canyon Village for Hamilton Stores; this trip fulfilled our desire to see the park in the winter; we had a wonderful time
- It is a magical place and we will be back; please don't make it any more commercial, or allow too many people in winter - thanks
- It is beautiful in the winter
- It is magnificent; continue to protect from visitor damage; enforce the rules
- It was a calming, enjoyable visit
- It was a good experience
- It was a great day - Pierre of Backcountry Adventures was very informative; spotted lots of animals, coyote, 5 bald eagles, bison, elk, etc. Need more than 1 ladies room at Madison junction in the winter; wasted a lot of time in bathroom line
- It was a great experience and winter in the park is a whole different world - don't let it disappear from our choices
- It was a great visit
- It was a wonderful experience - sorry for tardy answer but illness and work came first; Xanterra does a wonderful job - keep them
- It was a wonderful vacation; we really enjoyed seeing Yellowstone in the winter
- It was an experience of a lifetime; very, very memorable
- It was fantastic - we camp in YNP every year and love it, but the winter visit was magical
- It was fun; we appreciated groomed ski trails
- It was great
- It was great and we would like to return every year
- It was great; the tour guide (Turtle) was informative and a great guide
- It was great; the winter weather was great

- It was the trip of a lifetime - Yellowstone in winter is fun
- It would have been nice if we were offered a 'welcome back' after being stuck for 3 hours - suggestion: appoint hosts/contact persons for group visitors
- It's awesome
- Just that we want to live there now and felt sad going home
- Keep it as it is. Do not open the roads in winter with snowplows. Keep it unique. Reduce the number of skimobiles. (No snowmobiles)
- Keep it for the people
- Keep snowmobiling alive in the park; it is way more not busy in the winter and provides a better experience that in the summer
- Keep up the good work
- Keep up the good work
- Loved it
- Loved the snowshoe tour at Old Faithful
- Loved the winter experience after visiting in Fall 2011, exceeded all expectations; a photographer's paradise
- More cellular coverage in park
- More information on signposts on ski tracks e.g. position, distance and better cell phone coverage for emergency use
- More or better lighting in lodge rooms; less waste of soap - possibly smaller bars - 3 is unnecessary
- More personal access - less guided tour. Park needs to allow more tours to enter park or lift restrictions on only guided tours or get more guides; I feel this drove up the overall tour cost; should have been about half what we paid
- More real bathrooms. Especially in winter need more heated restrooms; not enough potties, stinky and cold
- More restrooms
- More restrooms
- More trails for snowshoeing and more of a "share the trail" campaign so that cross country skiers don't take/get the whole trail with all others crammed off to soft, unstable edges. Current campaign is - these trails are for skiers - all others get off to the side - or go away (this seems to be the preference)
- More women stalls in rest areas
- Need "one" tag for our personal snowmobiles between Montana and Idaho - we visit both areas
- Need more gift shops and restaurants open
- Needs to stay open in the winter
- Nicely groomed trails for skiing. Friendly service staff
- No - everything was good
- No rational basis for not letting individual snowmobiles in park; animal population has declined since limits
- Nope, great visit
- Offer a blend - if we stay outside park, have opportunity to participate in Ranger programs
- Old Faithful Snow Lodge is an excellent hotel - love it that there are no TVs in any hotels
- Outstanding experience
- Outstanding staff at Snow Lodge registration and restaurant
- Overall was great! Cross country skiing incredible! Enjoy peace, quiet and few motors. Loud motors ruin the experience.

o Park rangers appeared to believe they owned the park and acted as though we were trespassing; I understand the need for a 4-stroke snowmobile, but I don't understand the reasoning for a guide

o Pattern the park like those in Canada

o Please continue to allow controlled snowmobile tours. Access to the park in winter is critical.

o Please continue to allow snowmobiles in the park; loved the wildlife and the way all the areas have been left untouched to admire

o Please keep snowmobile access to the park

o Please protect the wildlife. We all have other places to live - they do not. Great trip. It would be great to have a few wheelchairs for checkout for people on crutches.

o Rangers at visitor center great. Wished someone had told me about toe warmers first day and sold them at visitor center. We enjoyed evening piano music, slide show at hotel, but he should consider updating it.

o Really value the snowcoach - provides access otherwise not possible

o Relative balance of snowcoach and snowmobile seemed about right - cooperative and respectful of each other; not too crowded so as to affect the quality of the visit

o Restaurants very good

o Retain the rustic/historic feel of the lodging

o Should allow car traffic into park at West Yellowstone; not just snowcoach/snowmobile admission; many people don't have $125/person for such things

o Signage to ski trails inadequate; ski trail maps didn't correlate to trail signs; Daisy trail from Biscuit Basin. Also, was impossible to find signage to Mystic Falls confusing compared to map

o Ski trails where not marked very good

o Snowmobiling is the best and safest way for seeing WY P in winter; snow coaches are loud and too fast

o So nice to see public and private working well together. Feels freer, less 'rule-ridden.' It's grown well since 1962.

o Some type of VIP or frequent visit credits; we love the park, promote visits to others that are not local. We are not yet Golden Eagles, but come at least one time per year and usually more and bring others, but expensive for us. Snowcoach for a local person who frequents park at least one time a year a bit overpriced compared to someone who has never been (perspective).

o Thank you - take care or all the wonderful places and the wildlife as you did the last 30 years

o Thank you for allowing snowmobiles, it was breathtaking

o Thanks

o That we loved it - Thanks

o The geysers in winter were fascinating; Michelle, our snowcoach driver (Yellowstone.com) was great - shared YNP history, wildlife information, recent events and more. We understand people experience YNP in different ways, however, to protect the park and wildlife and recreational experience of all visitors, snowmobile should not be more than 350/day - tours should remain guided only

o The gift shop at Old Faithful needs to be updated with newer styles of things that appeal to younger

o The greeting/registration at Snow Lodge was not helpful when our rooms were not ready, when asked about where we could store our luggage while we enjoyed our walk

o The music at Mammoth was unexpected and lovely; also snowcoach driver (Daniel) extremely knowledgeable

o The price of the Frosty Fun packages could be listed more clearly on the website depending on the lodging choice. Upon check-in include information on the ranger talks at 7:30. We were planning on being dropped at Fairy Falls our 2nd and last morning. When we tried to make a reservation the day before we were told there was a large group using all the snow coaches and there were none available. If we'd been told the day before when we first inquired about trips we would've gone the day before and reversed our plans. With that large of a trip, the staff must have known. We were disappointed to miss the trip.

o   The shuttle for skiing was very important and we rated it very good

o   The signage for ski trails in the park was excellent; extremely helpful. Many of our group really like the Bombadier snow coaches and hope to see them continue in service

o   The snowmobiles needed work on the suspension, very rough ride was unnecessary with proper maintenance

o   The snowshoe tour was the best and we went to all the ranger talks; The Mammoth Hot Springs Hotel was too hot; The young ranger at Mammoth was excellent; Orville, the ranger at Old Faithful should remove the slide of the burned bison being slaughtered by the bear - Grizzly indeed; Thank you for minimizing noise and invasiveness of snowmobiles. Please protect the wolves and balance of nature - Thank you

o   The staff are very friendly and accommodating; we love the free-roaming wildlife

o   The trip was all that we expected and more

o   The trip was the greatest

o   The Yellowstone Association does an excellent job representing the NPS and Yellowstone Park

o   There were too few winter related recreation opportunities available to families of average means, within the park itself

o   This has been a winter of little snow. It would have been great to open other roads based on road conditions

o   This was a part of a "Bucket List" for my elderly, but very active mother - we had a wonderful experience

o   This was my first snowcoach tour and first winter visit to the park and it was fantastic

o   Totally enjoyed

o   Vehicles pulling snowmobiles are extremely rude, careless drivers; they speed down the Lamar without a care or consideration of the wildlife

o   Very enjoyable

o   Very enjoyable, friendly staff

o   Visit was great - this questionnaire is too long and confusing. We were with a tour group, so nothing was booked individually

o   Visit was great, informative trip. Plan on re-visiting at a later date, maybe fall season. All staff was very nice and helpful.

o   Visitor center at Old Faithful is really nice, skiing was fantastic, it's great that there are less snow machines - keep the park as natural as you can. Loved the skate-ski groomed trails around lodge staff at Snow Lodge were very friendly and helpful

o   Visitor Center at Old Faithful was nice and appropriate

o   Visits to specific thermal features were outstanding; loved the bison and eagles and their nests

o   We absolutely loved it! We just felt money spent for snowcoach was too expensive for us

o   We are very concerned about the policy of Yellowstone National Park regarding wolves. The elk population is declining dramatically and we are concerned few if any elk will survive. The wolves should be reduced in number. They are having an unfortunate negative impact on elk, moose and buffalo calves in the park. This may impact visitor numbers if not reversed; our guests were very disappointed at the small number of elk that were observed. It is clear the wolves are growing in number with unfortunate consequences.

o   We can't wait to come back

o   We did not like having to travel with a guide; we are quite capable of finding our way around and could have preferred to travel where we wanted to go

o   We do not want the government to ban snowmobiles in the park; all the traffic in the summer puts off more pollution than the snowmobiles in winter

o   We feel fortunate that the winter yurts are available at Canyon Camp - they are the reason we visit

o   We felt that snowmobiling was an awesome way for a family who is able to experience the park and the beauty of Yellowstone and to really feel a part of the elements. Tours and additional maps should be available in other major languages.

o   We had a great time

o   We had a great time

o   We had a great time; the park employees and Xanterra employees were all very pleasant and helpful

o   We had a great tour

o   We had a great tour (snowcoach tour out of West Yellowstone) of the park - the park is beautiful in winter

o   We had Rendezvous snowmobile and Matt as our guide; he was very knowledgeable and had a passion for the park; it was refreshing to see someone like their job and be great at it

o   We hope to visit again soon

o   We like the limit on snowmobiles; our guide was very caring of the wildlife and went out of her way to not stress them (Alice at Alpine Guides)

o   We love coming every year; please keep this natural wonder as primitive as possible

o   We love the park; we don't do big tours - at this point there are so many visitors that we only come in the winter. The quality of the facilities is poor, the services average and the recreational opportunities are fabulous

o   We love Yellowstone during all seasons

o   We loved it

o   We loved it! Yellowstone Vacations had great tour guides who taught us a lot. It was good to see the park in its winter state. Please keep these snowcoaches going - everyone should experience this.

o   We loved the skiing; hanging out in lobby of Snow Lodge, free ice skating for kids, ranger talks, etc.

o   We really missed live music in the Snowlodge on Tues and Wed - present on our visit 4 years ago and visits to Mammoth past 3 years

o   We used the ski drop service. Really enjoyed this service as it opens up more of the park to see and ski. Also, enjoyed hot tubbing at night. Please put a rail around the ice skating rink so those of us who are not good ice skaters can have a rail to hold onto. Thanks. Park employees are very friendly and informative. Always enjoy visiting with them.

o   We visited on 2/18-20/2012 - this makes a big difference in the cost of lodging outside the park and what areas are available within the park; hopefully you're considering seasonal factors - thanks

o   We were glad to see the store open during winter season since we didn't expect it; also, the bathroom at Mammoth were very clean

o   We were not prepared for effects of dry climate and high altitude

o   We will be back

o   We wish we could have spent more time to see more

o   We work within 150 miles

o   We would have liked an evening program on Sunday - it was a 3-day weekend - thanks

o   We would like to have had some sort of organized activity inside the snow lodge; example lecture, movie, music

o   We would like to visit the park in the winter by use of personal snowmobiles and without a guide to enjoy it at our own pace; the winter wildlife viewing has been impacted too much by the wolves.

o   West Yellowstone, MT is convenient base of operations but could not find any connection from West Yellowstone to concessionaires; otherwise we might have used a concession service

o   While in the park, I needed to take care of some urgent business; I appreciated that I could access the internet in the privacy of my room, even though there was a fee

o   Will definitely come back

- Wish we could snowmobile without a guide
- Wished the facilities we wanted were available for a short visit to the park in the winter; we loved the Alpen Snowcoach tour
- Wolf tour should make more effort to find wolves or be less expensive and just called Scenic Lamar Valley Tour
- Wonderful opportunity to compare winter with summer; extremely important to have YNP open in the winter, including providing jobs and winter services
- Would love to return to the Snow Lodge at Old Faithful
- WOW
- YA runs great programs - we'll be back
- Yellowstone exceeded our expectations - the diversity of interesting features, from wildlife to scenery and geology, there was something unexpected around every corner
- Yellowstone in the winter was an unknown gem - we will definitely return
- Yes, the wildlife was fabulous

Appendix 1: The Questionnaire

United States Department of the Interior

NATIONAL PARK SERVICE
Yellowstone National Park
Yellowstone NP, WY 82190

IN REPLY REFER TO

July 2011

Dear Visitor:

Thank you for participating in this important study. Our goal is to learn about the expectations, opinions, and interests of visitors to Yellowstone National Park. This information will assist us in our efforts to better manage this park and to serve you.

This questionnaire is only being given to a select number of visitors, so your participation is very important. It should only take about 20 minutes to complete after your visit.

When your visit is over, please complete this questionnaire. Seal it in the postage-paid envelope provided and drop it in any U.S. mailbox.

If you have any questions, please contact Margaret Littlejohn, NPS VSP Director, Park Studies Unit, College of Natural Resources, P.O. Box 441139, University of Idaho, Moscow, Idaho 83844-1139, phone: 208-885-7863, email: littlej@uidaho.edu.

We appreciate your help.

Sincerely,

Daniel N. Wenk
Superintendent

Social Science Division
National Park Service
U.S. Department of the Interior

Visitor Services Project

Yellowstone National Park

Visitor Study

Your Visit To Yellowstone National Park

NOTE: In this questionnaire "personal group" is defined as anyone with whom you are visiting the park, such as a spouse, family, friends, etc. This does not include the larger group that you might be traveling with, such as school, church, scout, or tour group.

1. a) Prior to this visit, how did you and your personal group obtain information about Yellowstone National Park (NP)? Please mark (●) **all that apply in column (a).**

   ○ Did not obtain information prior to visit → **Go to part (b) of this question**

   b) If you were to visit Yellowstone NP in the future, how would you and your personal group prefer to obtain information about the park? Please mark (●) **all that apply in column (b).**

a) This visit	b) Future visit	Source of information
○	○	Friends/relatives/word of mouth
○	○	Inquiry to park via phone, mail, or email
○	○	Local businesses (airport, hotels, motels, restaurants, etc.)
○	○	Maps/brochures
○	○	Newspaper/magazine articles
○	○	Previous visits
○	○	School class/program
○	○	Social media (e.g., Facebook, Twitter, etc.)
○	○	State welcome center/visitors bureau/chamber of commerce
○	○	Television/radio programs/DVDs
○	○	Travel guides/tour books (such as AAA, etc.)
○	○	Yellowstone NP website: www.nps.gov/yell
○	○	Xanterra concession website: www.travelyellowstone.com
○	○	Delaware North concession website: www.delawarenorth.com
○	○	Other websites
○	n/a	Other, this visit (Specify) _____
n/a	○	Other, future visit (Specify) _____

DIRECTIONS

At the end of your visit:

1. Please have the selected individual (at least 16 years old) complete this questionnaire.

2. Answer the questions carefully since each question is different.

3. For questions that use circles (○), please mark your answer by filling in the circle with **black or blue ink**. Please do not use pencil!

   Like this: ●   Not like this: ⊘ ⊗ ⊘ ⊙

4. Seal it in the postage-paid envelope provided.

5. Drop it in a U.S. mailbox.

Paperwork Reduction Act Statement: The Paperwork Reduction Act requires us to tell you why we are collecting this information, how we will use it, and whether or not you have to respond. This information will be used by the National Park Service as authorized by 16 U.S.C. 1a-7. We will use this information to evaluate visitor services cooperatively managed by Yellowstone National Park. Your response is voluntary. Your name and address have been requested for follow-up purposes only. At the completion of this collection all names and personal information will be destroyed and in no way be connected with the results of this survey. A Federal agency may not conduct or sponsor and you are not required to respond to a collection of information unless it displays a currently valid OMB Control Number. We estimate that it will take an average of 20 minutes to complete the survey associated with this collection of information. You may send comments concerning the burden estimates or any aspect of this information collection to Margaret Littlejohn, NPS Visitor Services Project, College of Natural Resources, University of Idaho, P.O. Box 441139, Moscow, ID, 83844-1139; email: littlej@uidaho.edu.

5. a) On this visit, how many times did you and your personal group enter Yellowstone NP during your stay in the area (within 150 miles)?

_____ Number of entries

b) Which entrances did you and your personal group use to enter the park? Please mark (●) all that apply. (See map on page 7.)

- ○ West Yellowstone
- ○ North Entrance (Gardiner)
- ○ South Entrance (Flagg Ranch)
- ○ Northeast Entrance (Cooke City)
- ○ East Entrance (Cody)

c) On this visit, how many vehicles did you and your personal group use to arrive at the park? Please write "0" if you did not arrive by vehicle.

_____ Number of vehicles

6. a) For this trip, please mark (●) all the park locations that you and your personal group visited in Yellowstone NP. If you did not visit a location, please leave that line blank. Use the map on the next page to help you identify the locations you visited.

b) & c) Please list the amount of time you spent at each location in hours or days. If you spent less than 24 hours, list the number of hours in column (b). If you spent 24 hours or more, list the number of days in column (c). Also list the total time spent in Yellowstone NP. List partial hours or days as 1/4, 1/2, 3/4.

a) Visited park location (●)	b) Hours spent—if less than 24 hours	c) Days spent—if 24 hours or more
○ Mammoth Hot Springs	_____	_____
○ Madison	_____	_____
○ Old Faithful	_____	_____
○ West Thumb/Grant Village	_____	_____
○ Fishing Bridge/Lake Village/ Bridge Bay	_____	_____
○ Tower-Roosevelt	_____	_____
○ Canyon Village	_____	_____
Total time spent in Yellowstone NP on this visit	_____	_____

d) Were you and your personal group able to visit all the locations in Yellowstone NP that you had planned to visit?

- ○ No
- ○ Yes → Go to Question 7

---

c) From the sources marked in column (a), did you and your personal group receive the type of information about the park that you needed?

- ○ No
- ○ Yes → Go to Question 2

d) If NO, what type of park information did you and your personal group need that was not available? Please be specific.

2. For this trip, what was the primary reason that you and your personal group visited the Yellowstone NP area (within 150 miles)? Please mark (●) only one.

- ○ Resident of area
- ○ Visit Yellowstone NP
- ○ Visit Grand Teton NP
- ○ Visit other attractions in the area
- ○ Traveling through - unplanned visit
- ○ Visit friends/relatives in the area
- ○ Other (Please specify) _____
- ○ Business
- ○ Fishing
- ○ Study natural history
- ○ Watch wildlife

3. On this visit, were the signs directing you and your personal group to and within Yellowstone NP adequate? Please mark (●) one answer for each of the following.

	Yes	No	Did not use
a) Interstate signs	○	○	○
b) State highway signs	○	○	○
c) National Park Service signs in developed areas of the park such as Old Faithful, Tower, Lake Village, etc.	○	○	○

4. a) In the park, did you and your personal group have any problem finding commercial services (such as lodging, food, gas, gift shops, etc.)?

- ○ Yes
- ○ No → Go to Question 5

b) If YES, which of the following reasons contributed to the problem? Please mark (●) all that apply.

- ○ Signs
- ○ Traffic circulation
- ○ Service was closed
- ○ Other (Specify) _____

b) If YES, please list the number of nights you and your personal group stayed.

_____ Number of nights inside Yellowstone NP

_____ Number of nights outside Yellowstone NP within 150 miles of park

c) & d) In which types of accommodations did you and your personal group spend the night(s)? Please mark (●) **all that apply.**

	c) **Inside park**	d) **Outside park within 150 miles**
Lodge, motel, cabin, rented condo/home, or bed & breakfast	○	○
➜ If you stayed **inside** the park, in what **type** of lodging? _____		
➜ If you stayed **inside** the park, at what **location?** _____		
Camping in developed campground	○	○
Backcountry campsite	○	○
Personal seasonal residence	○	○
Residence of friends or relatives	○	○
Other (Please specify below)	○	○

Inside _____ Outside _____

8. On this trip, where did you and your personal group stay on the **night before** and the **night after** visiting Yellowstone NP? If you stayed at home, please write the name of the town/city and state where you live.

a) BEFORE visit: Town/city _____ State _____

b) AFTER visit: Town/city _____ State _____

9. a) On this visit, did you and your personal group visit the Old Faithful Inn?

○ Yes   ○ No

b) On this visit, did you and your personal group stay overnight at the Old Faithful Inn?

○ Yes   ○ No

e) If NO, why not? _____

f) Which locations were you and your personal group unable to visit?

_____

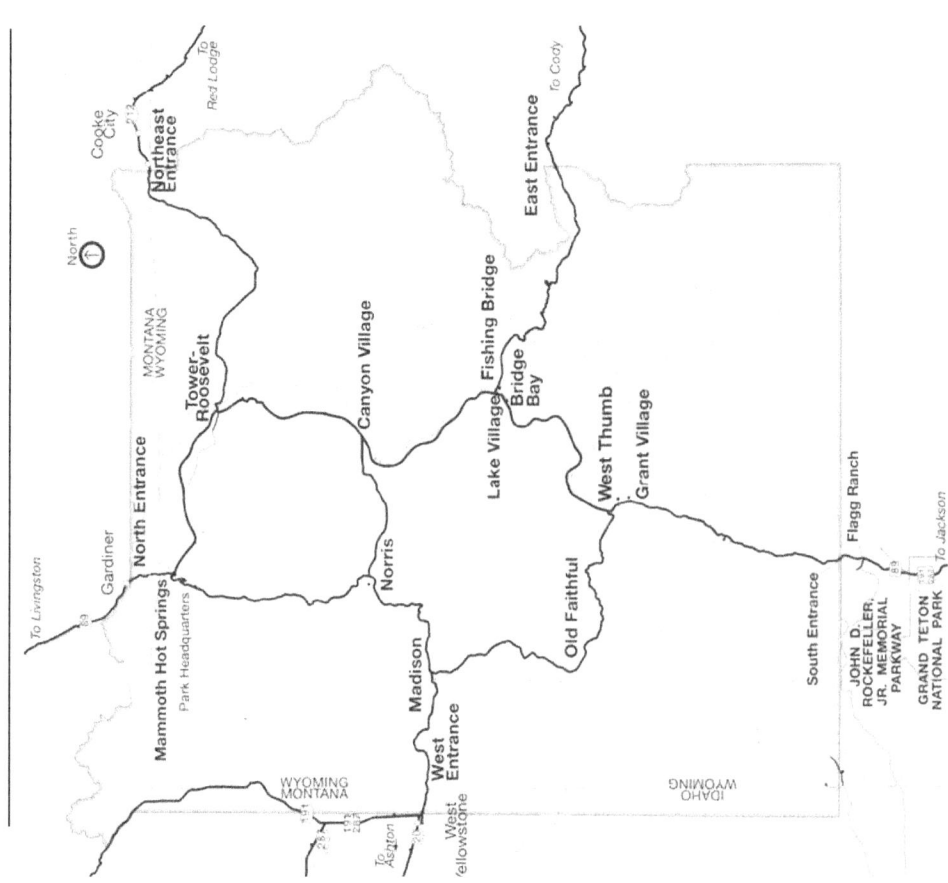

7. a) On this trip, did you and your personal group stay **overnight away from home** in Yellowstone NP or in the area within 150 miles of any entrance point?

○ Yes   ○ No ➜ **Go to Question 8**

10. a) On this visit, in which activities did you and your personal group participate within Yellowstone NP? Please mark (●) **all** that apply.

○ Attending ranger-led programs

○ Boardwalk/geyser basin

○ Camping in developed campgrounds

○ Creative arts (painting/drawing/photography/writing)

○ Day hiking

○ Eating in park restaurants

○ Overnight backpacking (camping in the backcountry)

○ Picnicking

○ Shopping in park bookstores

○ Shopping in park stores (gift shops and general stores)

○ Sightseeing/taking a scenic drive

○ Staying in park lodging

○ Viewing roadside/trailside exhibits

○ Viewing wildlife/birdwatching

○ Visiting park visitor center(s)/museum(s)　How many did you visit? _____

○ Other (Please specify) _____

b) Which **one** of the above activities was the primary reason you and your personal group visited Yellowstone NP on this visit? Please list **only one** response.

_____

11. On a future visit, would you and your group like to have the following services available in developed areas in Yellowstone NP?

a) Cell phone　　　　○ Yes　　○ No

b) Internet access　　○ Yes　　○ No

c) Other (Please specify) _____

NOTE: Commercial services at Yellowstone NP include lodging, food, camping, gas stations, gift shops and medical services that are provided by concessionaires such as Xanterra, Delaware North, etc.

12. a) On this visit to Yellowstone NP, which of the following commercial services did you and personal your group use? Please mark (●) **all** that apply.

b) If you and your personal group used lodging, campgrounds and/or restaurants/food services, were you able to get your first choice of location?

c) Did the commercial services that you and personal your group used meet your expectations? Please circle one.

d) Please rate the value (from 1 to 5) of the commercial services you and personal your group used, for the money you paid.

a) Service used (●)	Commercial service in Yellowstone NP	b) Did you get your first choice? (Circle one)		c) Meet expectations? 1=Worse than expected 2=About what was expected 3=Better than expected (Circle one)			d) Value for money you paid 1=Very poor 2=Poor 3=Average 4=Good 5=Very good
○	Lodging	Yes	No	1	2	3	_____
○	Campgrounds	Yes	No	1	2	3	_____
○	Restaurants/food service	Yes	No	1	2	3	_____
○	Purchase gas	n/a		1	2	3	_____
○	Purchase gifts/ souvenirs	n/a		1	2	3	_____
○	Medical services	n/a		1	2	3	_____

e) If you marked "No" or "Worse than expected" to part (b) or (c) of this question, please explain where and why.

Location _____　Reason _____

_____

f) If you marked "Very poor" or "Poor" in part (d) of this question please explain where and why.

Location _____　Reason _____

_____

g) If you marked "Very good" in part (d) of this question, please explain.

_____

14. For you and your personal group, please report all expenditures for the items listed below for this visit to Yellowstone NP and the surrounding area (within 150 miles of any entrance point). **Please write "0" if no money was spent in a particular category.**

a) Please list your personal group's total expenditures inside Yellowstone NP.

b) Please list your group's total expenditures outside the park (within 150 miles).

NOTE: Surrounding area residents should only include expenditures that were just for this visit to Yellowstone NP.

EXPENDITURES

	a) Inside park	b) Outside park
	O → Go to (b)	O → Go to (c)
Spent no money (●)	O → Go to (b)	O → Go to (c)
Lodges, hotels, motels, cabins, B&Bs, etc.	$	$
Camping fees and charges	$	$
Guide fees and charges	$	$
Restaurants and bars	$	$
Groceries and takeout food	$	$
Gas and oil (auto, RV, boat, etc.)	$	$
Other transportation expenses (including airfare, rental cars, auto repairs, etc.)	$	$
Fishing/boating	$	$
Admission, recreation, entertainment fees	$	$
All other purchases (souvenirs, film, books, sporting goods, clothing, etc.)	$	$
Donations	$	$

c) How many people do the above expenses cover?

_____ Adults (18 years or over) _____ Children (under 18 years)
Please write "0" if no children were covered by the expenditures.

15. On this visit, were you and your personal group part of the following types of organized groups? Please mark (●) **one** for each.

		Yes	No
a) Commercial guided tour group		O Yes	O No
b) School/educational group		O Yes	O No
c) Other (business, church, scouts, work)		O Yes	O No

d) If you were with one of these organized groups, how many people, including yourself, were in this group?

_____ Number of people in organized group

---

13. a) Prior to your visit to Yellowstone NP, which concession services and activities did you or your personal group plan to do, or make reservations for, before arrival? Please mark (●) **all** that apply.

b) Please mark (●) **all** the concession services and activities that you or personal your group **used** during this visit to Yellowstone NP.

c) Next, for **only** those services and activities that you or your personal group **used**, please rate their importance to your visit from 1-5.

d) Finally, for **only** those services and activities that you or your personal group **used**, please rate their quality from 1-5.

a) Concession service/ activity planned or reserved in Yellowstone NP before visit?	b) Concession service/ activity used in Yellowstone NP on this visit	c) If used, how important? 1=Not at all important 2=Slightly important 3=Moderately important 4=Very important 5=Extremely important	d) If used, what quality? 1=Very poor 2=Poor 3=Average 4=Good 5=Very good
O	Bicycle tour	_____	_____
O	Boat rental	_____	_____
O	Cookout	_____	_____
O	Guided canoe/kayak trip	_____	_____
O	Guided fishing trip	_____	_____
O	Guided hiking trip	_____	_____
O	Guided overnight backpacking trip	_____	_____
O	Guided overnight horse pack trip	_____	_____
O	Natural history tour (not ranger-guided)	_____	_____
O	Photography tour	_____	_____
O	Scenic boat tour	_____	_____
O	Scenic motorized tour	_____	_____
O	Trail ride	_____	_____
O	Stagecoach ride	_____	_____
O	Yellowstone Association Institute class	_____	_____

c) What **services** in the park need to be provided in languages other than English? Please specify a service(s) or mark (●) "None."

○ None

○ Service(s) _____

20. a) Does anyone in your personal group have a physical condition that made it difficult to access or participate in park activities or services?

○ Yes   ○ No **→ Go on to Question 21**

b) If YES, what services or activities were difficult to access/participate in? _____

c) Because of the physical condition, which specific difficulties did the person(s) have? Please mark (●) **all** that apply.

○ Hearing (difficulty hearing ranger programs, bus drivers, audio-visual exhibits or programs, or information desk staff, even with hearing aid)

○ Visual (difficulty seeing exhibits, directional signs, or visual aids that are part of programs, even with prescribed glasses, or due to blindness)

○ Mobility (difficulty accessing facilities, services, or programs, even with walking aid and/or wheelchair)

○ Other (Please specify) _____

21. a) Are you or members of your personal group Hispanic or Latino? Please mark (●) **one** for each group member.

	Yourself	Member #2	Member #3	Member #4	Member #5	Member #6	Member #7
Yes, Hispanic or Latino	○	○	○	○	○	○	○
No, not Hispanic or Latino	○	○	○	○	○	○	○

b) What is your race? What is the race of each member of your personal group? Please mark (●) **one or more** for you and each group member.

	Yourself	Member #2	Member #3	Member #4	Member #5	Member #6	Member #7
American Indian or Alaska Native	○	○	○	○	○	○	○
Asian	○	○	○	○	○	○	○
Black or African American	○	○	○	○	○	○	○
Native Hawaiian or other Pacific Islander	○	○	○	○	○	○	○
White	○	○	○	○	○	○	○

16. a) On this visit, what type of personal group (not guided tour/school/other organized group) were you with? Please mark (●) **one.**

○ Alone   ○ Friends

○ Family   ○ Family and friends

○ Other (Please specify) _____

b) On this visit, how many people were in your personal group, including yourself?

_____ Number of people in personal group

17. For you and your personal group on this visit, please provide the following. If you do not know the answer, leave blank.

	a) Gender M=Male F=Female	b) Current age	c) U.S. ZIP code or name of country other than U.S.	Number of visits to Yellowstone NP (including this visit) d) Past 12 months	e) **Lifetime**
Yourself	_____	_____	_____	_____	_____
Member #2	_____	_____	_____	_____	_____
Member #3	_____	_____	_____	_____	_____
Member #4	_____	_____	_____	_____	_____
Member #5	_____	_____	_____	_____	_____
Member #6	_____	_____	_____	_____	_____
Member #7	_____	_____	_____	_____	_____

18. For you only, what is the highest level of education you have completed? Please mark (●) **one.**

○ Some high school   ○ Bachelor's degree

○ High school diploma/GED   ○ Graduate degree

○ Some college

19. a) & b) When visiting an area such as Yellowstone NP, which language(s) do you and most members of your personal group prefer to use for the following?

a) Speaking: ○ English ○ Other (Specify) _____

b) Reading: ○ English ○ Other (Specify) _____

Yellowstone National Park Visitor Study 15

22. a) Which category best represents your annual **household** income? Please mark
(●) **one.**

○ Less than $24,999   ○ $150,000-$199,999
○ $25,000-$34,999   ○ $50,000-$74,999   ○ $200,000 or more
○ $35,000-$49,999   ○ $75,000-$99,999   ○ Do not wish to answer
   ○ $100,000-$149,999

b) How many people are in your household? _____ Number of people

23. a) Commercial services at Yellowstone NP include lodging, restaurants/food
service, stores, gift shops, medical clinics, gas stations, etc. On this visit, what
did you and your personal group like **most** about the commercial services?

_____

_____

b) On this visit, what did you and your personal group like **least** about the
commercial services (lodging, restaurants/food service, stores, gift shops,
medical clinics, gas stations, etc.) in Yellowstone NP?

_____

_____

24. Is there anything else you and your personal group would I ke to tell us about your
visit to Yellowstone NP?

_____

_____

_____

25. Overall, how would you rate the quality of the facilities, services, and recreational
opportunities provided to you and your personal group at Yellowstone NP during
this visit? Please mark (●) **one.**

Very poor   Poor   Average   Good   Very good
   ○   ○   ○   ○   ○

Thank you for your help! Please seal the questionnaire in the postage paid-envelope
provided and drop it in any U.S. mailbox.   ♲ Printed on recycled paper

PO 1139

Appendix 2: Additional Analysis

The Visitor Services Project (VSP) offers the opportunity to learn from VSP visitor study data through additional analysis. Two-way and three-way cross tabulations can be made with any questions.

Below are some examples of the types of cross tabulations that can be requested. To make a request, please use the contact information below, and include your name, address and phone number in the request.

1. What proportion of family groups with children attends interpretive programs?

2. Is there a correlation between visitors' ages and their preferred sources of information about the park?

3. Are highly satisfied visitors more likely to return for a future visit?

4. How many international visitors participate in hiking?

5. What ages of visitors would use the park website as a source of information on a future visit?

6. Is there a correlation between visitor groups' rating of the overall quality of their park experience and their ratings of individual services and facilities?

7. Do larger visitor groups (e.g., four or more) participate in different activities than smaller groups?

8. Do frequent visitors rate the overall quality of their park experiences differently than less frequent visitors?

The VSP database website (http://vsp.uidaho.edu) allows data searches for comparisons of data from one or more parks.

For more information please contact:

Visitor Services Project, PSU
College of Natural Resources
P.O. Box 441139
University of Idaho
Moscow, ID 83843-1139

Phone: 208-885-2585
Fax: 208-885-4261
Email: lenale@uidaho.edu
Website: http://www.psu.uidaho.edu

Appendix 3: Decision Rules for Checking Non-response Bias

There are several methods for checking non-response bias. However, the most common way is to use some demographic indicators to compare between respondents and non-respondents (Dey 1997; Salant and Dillman 1994; Dillman and Carley-Baxter 2000; Dillman, 2007; Stoop 2004). In this study, group type, group size, age of the group member (at least 16 years old) completing the survey, whether the park was the primary destination, and respondent's place of residence were five variables that were used to check for non-response bias.

Two independent-sample T-tests were used to test the differences between respondents and non-respondents. The p-values represent the significance levels of these tests. If the p-value is greater than 0.05, the two groups are judged to be insignificantly different.

Chi-square tests were used to detect the difference in the group types, whether the park is the primary reason for being in the area, and respondent's place of residence. The hypotheses were there would be no significant difference between respondents and non-respondents in terms of who they travelled with, why they were in the area, or where they came from. If the p-value is greater than 0.05, the differences are judged to be insignificant.

The hypotheses for checking non-response bias are: Respondents and non-respondents are not significantly difference in term of

1. Average age
2. Number of people they were travelling with in a personal group
3. Type of group which they were travelling with
4. Park as primary destination
5. Proximity from home to the park

As shown in Tables 3-6, respondents and non-respondents were not significantly different in terms of group size, group type, and park as primary destination. The p-values for respondent/non-respondent average age and proximity from home to the park are less than 0.05, indicating significant difference between respondents and non-respondents. The results indicated younger respondents (under 40 years old) may be underrepresented. Visitors who lived within 200 miles of the park may also be underrepresented in the results.

References

Dey, E. L. (1997). Working with Low Survey Response Rates: The Efficacy of Weighting Adjustment. *Research in Higher Education*, 38(2): 215-227.

Dillman, D. A. (2007). *Mail and Internet Surveys: The Tailored Design Method, Updated version with New Internet, Visual, and Mixed-Mode Guide*, 2nd Edition, New York: John Wiley and Sons, Inc.

Dillman, D. A. and Carley-Baxter, L. R. (2000). *Structural determinants of survey response rate over a 12-year period, 1988-1999*, Proceedings of the section on survey research methods, 394-399, American Statistical Association, Washington, D.C.

Filion, F. L. (Winter 1975-Winter 1976). Estimating Bias due to Non-response in Mail Surveys. *Public Opinion Quarterly*, Vol 39 (4): 482-492.

Goudy, W. J. (1976). Non-response Effect on Relationships Between Variables. *Public Opinion Quarterly*. Vol 40 (3): 360-369.

Mayer, C. S. and Pratt Jr. R. W. (Winter 1966-Winter 1967). A Note on Non-response in a Mail Survey. *Public Opinion Quarterly*. Vol 30 (4): 637-646.

Salant, P. and Dillman, D. A. (1994). *How to Conduct Your Own Survey*. U.S.: John Wiley and Sons, Inc.

Stoop, I. A. L. (2004). Surveying Non-respondents. *Field Methods*, 16 (1): 23.

NPS 101/119336, December 2012